CALIXTHE BEYALA was born in Cameroon, the sixth of a family of twelve children. She spent her childhood and adolescence in the shanty-town of New-Bell in Douala.

Now living in Paris, where she gained her degree, Beyala is a full-time writer and has enjoyed much success with her novels: *C'est le soleil qui m'a brûlée*, *Le petit prince de Belleville*, and *Seul le diable savait* as well as *Tu t'appelleras Tanga*, here translated into English for the first time.

A firm supporter of women's liberation, Calixthe Beyala describes herself as having 'a passion: Africa'.

MARJOLIJN de JAGER has a PhD in Romance Languages and Literatures from the University of North Carolina – Chapel Hill. She presently lives in New York where she teaches French at the Beacon High School. Her translations from both the French and the Dutch are numerous and have won many plaudits. She gives her special interest as francophone African literature, particularly written by women.

CALIXTHE BEYALA

YOUR NAME SHALL
BE TANGA

Translated from the French by
Marjolijn de Jager

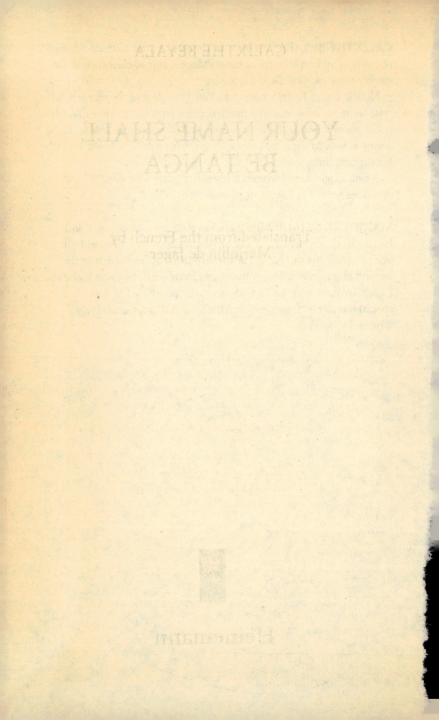

Heinemann

CALIXTHE BEYALA

YOUR NAME SHALL
BE TANGA

Translated from the French by
Marjolijn de Jager

Heinemann

The translator would like to dedicate her work on the novel to the memory of Mimi Guéye Ndoye, her colleague in love of literature and translation, her friend and sister in Dakar, met too late for the bud of friendship to come to a full bloom, yet the spirit of her being remains.

Heinemann Educational Publishers
A Division of Heinemann Publishers (Oxford) Ltd
Halley Court, Jordan Hill, Oxford OX2 8EJ

Heinemann: A Division of Reed Publishing (USA) Inc.
361 Hanover Street, Portsmouth, NH 03801–3912, USA

Heinemann Educational Books (Nigeria) Ltd
PMB 5205, Ibadan

Heinemann Educational Botswana Publishers (Pty) Ltd
PO Box 10103, Village Post Office, Gaborone, Botswana

FLORENCE PRAGUE PARIS MADRID
ATHENS MELBOURNE JOHANNESBURG
AUCKLAND SINGAPORE TOKYO
CHICAGO SÃO PAULO

First published in 1988 by Editions Stock as *Tu t'appelleras Tanga*
First published by Heinemann Educational Publishers in 1996

British Library Cataloguing in Publication Data
A catalogue record for this book is available from the British Library.

ISBN 0 435 909 509

Cover design by Touchpaper
Cover illustration by Jane Human
Author photograph by S. Haskell

Photoset by CentraCet Limited, Cambridge
Printed and bound in Great Britain
by Cox & Wyman Ltd, Reading, Berks

96 97 98 99 8 7 6 5 4 3 2 1

To Edwy, the child

I am going to die, woman. White people die as well you know? To dive into death as you do into life. Without a visa, without a passport. What can you do? Death is copious and complex. You can add it up, multiply it, and display its deductions, the same way a merchant does with his books. For a long time I refused to get mixed up in its calculations. What I wanted to do was to change the world. Leave with my belongings rolled up in a plastic bag under my arm. Leave for places that have neither earth nor heaven. To look for the blind one. He will read the holy book of life to me. He will speak to me of Bangkok, Dar-es-Salaam, Mississippi, Kilimanjaro, Cheops. I will take over his shift; I will go without seeing, with open eyes, and I will see when my eyes are closed. I will go and find the madwoman. In the rain I'll close my umbrella and I'll open it in the desert. I'll go and find the child locked in innocence. He'll travel inside my memory: 'I am you, you are me, we are one.' I'll rob unhappiness. I'll attain peace. And there'll be the man from Japan filming every one of his meals. There'll be the little girl skipping rope and the man watching her with a smile. But death is there. She prowls all around this prison. Without permission! Nobody asks for my opinion. Besides I haven't any. Poor mortal and a woman into the bargain. It's not for me to forbid nor to give permission. Fear? Who's talking about fear? Fear is an illusion. As is man. As is God. Even he knows fear. I see him sitting on his cloud of dust, trembling at the thought of blowing the wind of knowledge into the world, or song or laughter, and finally setting the wheel of love going. What can I, woman, do about that? My death exists before I do, and well beyond me. That's God's way – his very personal way – of getting rid of all undesirables. Otherwise, he'd die poisoned, killed by his own work.

◆

1

Anna-Claude is silent and throws a neutral look at the young girl lying on the ground. In the frail light, her skin seems even blacker. Her frizzy hair, drenched in sweat, looks like the vomit of a disembowelled armchair. Her lips, split open from hunger, move forward with slow steps towards the antechamber to the struggle with death. Death has already ploughed its furrows in the motionless body. Only the eyes have the pungency of a violent hate that's hooked on an existence of silence and unfinished gestures.

It was early in the week that the cops dragged her here, breathless, her body dripping sweat and blood. Anna-Claude had bent over her, taken her pulse which was weakening, dressed her wounds with a piece of fabric taken from her dress and had asked her for her name. The unknown woman had said: 'My memory has closed itself to that. Let my steps move into the darkness without leaving any trace. What should it matter to you? Let me leave this life without disturbing the sleep of men.' She lay curled up in a corner and refused any gesture, any word, any food.

Anna-Claude had made every effort to speak to her. But to no avail. She had told her her own life story, up to the moment when their paths had crossed, up to the time of her madness and the death she was coming to glean in Africa. She had told the woman of Anna-Claude the paranoiac.

On the walls of her Paris apartment, she would draw menacing faces to exorcise the pain of living. She'd get up in the middle of the night, naked, her eyes stinging with sleep, go from the living room to the kitchen looking for the face of the monster that was haunting her rest. Where could the evil be coming from? From the city noises? From her? From others? Or quite simply from the exasperating calm that had been reigning for forty years, since the end of her childhood, since the end of the war. No answer. Her body was drying up. Deep wrinkles were carving into her forehead. And in her gaze always the same questions – always that bewildered look of a child.

When the time for class arrived, she'd go to meet her students again, with haggard eyes and unkempt hair. She'd sit on top of the front desk, with her chest pushed out, and she'd speak. Decisive, hard, mysterious. A teacher of philosophy, she would sacrifice Hegel and Kant to the occult sciences. She'd endlessly affirm that the

2

meeting point of the world lay in the imaginary and that it would suffice to close one's eyes, to listen to one's own vibrations to reach it. She'd talk about the Africa of the evil eye, fetishers and marabouts. She'd affirm it, retract, then affirm herself by affirming them. She'd talk about herself by talking about them, about a place in Africa where she was supposed to have lived in a previous life; about a husband she was supposed to have buried alive for having desecrated faithfulness, about her twelve children, two of whom had died. The students would listen to her, laugh, and murmur that she was crazy. Her friends did the same.

She really was mad. The kind of madness which asked questions without ever replying, which created time and stopped it, claimed kinship with every place in the world where man abolished frontiers. The frontiers remained, her madness continued.

Anna-Claude? She had fallen apart. She would spend her free days concocting birthday cakes for the demons who hunted down her repose. She'd walk the streets, invite people round, dozens of people she encountered by chance. She said that chance didn't exist and that if she ran across them, it was because the stars willed it so. She dwelled on the same old stories, touched them up in order to shut the doors of her distress, in order to turn the wheels of laughter. And the people around her laughed, made fun of her. They'd run into her in the streets, the cafés, at friends' houses; they'd say: 'What's new, Anna-Claude?' She'd dive into words, set up questions, build theories. Whether they listened or not, she'd continue. When she had reached her limits and could talk no more, she'd recommend reading material and exhort them to think about their future.

Anna-Claude! For the time being, she'd invented her man. Fashioned to fit her dreams. She called him Ousmane. He was handsome, he was tall, he was smart. He lived in Africa where he was building bridges and roads and soon he'd be returning to her in their Paris apartment. In her visions she imagined him. He would appear wearing a white *boubou* and blue pleated trousers. He would say:

'Woman, I saw you on the shores of my dreams. Then you disappeared.'

3

'I was waiting for you, woman. I was waiting for you and I
was afraid that death would cut me down while I was waiting.'

'I lived in emptiness; only the absence of your womb; only
your absence.'

'Remember, woman, remember us before time began, when I
was neither you nor me.'

'Remember still more. I was river and you a plant, oblivious
in the rocking of my arms. We used to sing until the day came
to an end, until midnight fell. Today, only the brook still
trembles.'

'Remember us – me inside you, and how with me still in
your wake we'd look at the sky, always at the sky to count the
moons.'

'You'd hold my hand and take me back to your home, your
origins. Everything depends on you, woman. Destiny depends
on you, gesture and oblivion depend on you.'

She was living his life and she used to speak to him. She told her
friends about his moods, his mannerisms, his refusal to speak until
he'd had two or three cups of coffee, the smell of his cigar. She kept
telling her stories; she believed in them. They had ended up by
believing her. She had made him a wardrobe inside her closet:
gandouras, striped shirts, matching socks, trousers and jackets. A
corner of her desk had been cleaned up for his work. In every room
of the apartment a variety of portraits showed him looking nonchal-
ant, energetic, laughing. She'd sit in front of the paintings for days
on end and would look at them until she was bleary-eyed. When she
received her friends at teatime, with her head leaning against the
back of an armchair she'd point to a painting: 'This one I painted
while we were staying with my parents in the Massif Central, that
one while on holiday in Normandy, and the other ...' She'd
explain and go into detail. She ended up by realising their importance
and she persisted in polishing them in such a way as to bring them
close to perfection. To the men who accosted her in the street, on
metro platforms, she'd say: 'I am married; I'm expecting a baby.'
They'd insist, she'd persist. She'd add another piece to this or that

4

rickety detail, polishing it up. She'd ended up by sculpting her sex in marble.

But the years passed by and Ousmane didn't show up. Whenever she ran across a black man in the street and couldn't bear to wait any longer for that which ceaselessly escaped her, she'd stop and invite him to a café. He'd accept. Between two beers, she'd ask him if he knew Ousmane. Some would shake their heads, others would ask for specifics, which she'd give. They would point out cousin what's-his-name. She'd go there, and make her eyes sparkle again to reawaken the fire of love. The flame wouldn't spark and she'd say: 'I've got the time wrong!' and continue her solitary quest.

Then one day she woke up with the feeling that the time of pointless meandering about had come to an end. She decided to go and join Ousmane. She asked for a transfer from the ministry. She was offered a post in this former French colony.

She devoted the first months of her appointment in the small high school on the west coast of Iningué to searching for Ousmane. Walking between sky and dust, she'd go around in the middle of the afternoon, looking under the baobab trees, in the market-places, giving the description of her man. Nobody matched it, nobody was supposed to. Battle-weary, she consulted mediums and seers. They spoke to her of the sovereign flight of man in space, of the eternal nature of their love, of heaven which would soon reunite them. Even the gods who were invoked couldn't deliver her man.

The search for Ousmane had worn her out a bit, traced new wrinkles on her forehead and on the back of her hands. But Anna-Claude was still beautiful from the dreams that carried her onward and she overcame her despair. She devoted her free afternoons to the local women she received at home. She'd sit down on the floor, always dressed in the same green dress, slightly soiled under the armpits, and listen to their problems, their joys, their loves. She'd listen to them and she learned their language, enjoyed analysing it, finding in the most common sounds a mystical resonance. Then the demonstrations erupted. Several of her students disappeared. Anna-Claude didn't understand, she would ask questions, some people shrugged, others hid behind gestures of ignorance, all of them sharing the fear. For several days she walked, without turning back, head down, her hands clasped behind her, scrutinising the ground to find the light. She understood then that clarification could only come from her, from her desire to clear the undergrowth of doubt. She retraced her steps and locked herself in. She wept for three days and two nights and bemoaned so much wasted love. Nobody was listening to her, nobody heard her. Since words had no echo any more, she decided to write. She bought a placard which she inscribed: 'WHERE ARE OUR CHILDREN? STRANGLED BY A BUTCHER!' She walked around all day long with the placard hanging from her neck. Men looked at it, read it and hurried along as if their lives were at stake. Shutters would close as she passed by, drawing curtains of silence throughout the town. Only some filthy street urchins, taking advantage of the forthrightness of those who know that their words carry no weight, followed her, yelling rhythmically: 'She is really crazy, she is really crazy!' Anna-Claude was arrested and thrown in prison. 'A subversive and uncontrollable element,' said the commissioner.

Then the silent unknown woman had joined her. Where did she come from? What crime was she involved in? Anna-Claude had posed these questions in a thousand different ways. She always found herself faced with the closed doors of thought, the wall of silence behind which the young girl had taken refuge. It was getting on Anna-Claude's nerves – she'd speak and despair, all the more so because she knew that from now on only words could feed her. Yards and yards of sentences were wrapped around her, were draped over her captivity. They were losing their original meaning, forming heaps of downy cotton to soften the death of the stars.

◆

'I don't know why I keep talking to you,' Anna-Claude says. 'You stink of death and you refuse to bequeath me your story. What kind of monster are you really? I'm going round in circles. Like the earth. Like it, I too am going mad. What do you want me to do, eh, tell me? Scream for help? What does it do for you to remain that way, sealed up inside yourself? You're going to die. I feel it, I know it. Give me your story. I am your deliverance. You have to assassinate that silence you drag behind you like dead skin. It would prevent you from turning in your grave. Give me your story. I'll embellish it for you, for myself. I'll paint it with all the colours of the rainbow. Give me your story and I'll pour out your dream.'

In the cell, now dark with shadow, Anna-Claude twists and turns, exposed to her anguish. Now an eagle, then a viper, a goose, a crab, she moves forward in words. In the name of unrealisable dreams. In the name of severed language. In the name of rejected souls. She speaks, pleading for words. Her speech flows, drowns the room and lies in wait for silence's death throes. A shower of words, disproportionate to her helplessness. Despair. Rage. Shred every envelope of suffering. Kill the emptiness of silence. Aching all over with words, exhausted by the wait, she lets herself flop down on the floor and closes her eyes.

In the middle of the night she opens them, wrenched from the body's surrender by the sound of moaning. It is the unknown woman. Anna-Claude rushes over:

'Speak to me. Tell me what's wrong.'

'Let me die in peace. Everything there is to know is already deposited within you.' She bites her lips, then: 'We are pursued by the same barbarous phantoms.'

'Give me the names; I'll pass them on. The rights of man do exist, you know?'

'Those who want to know must search and find. All you have to do is look.'

'How do you want me to manage that? I'm a foreigner here; have you forgotten?'

'Well then, enter into me. My secret will be illuminated. But first, the white woman in you must die. Give me your hand; from now on you shall be me. You shall be seventeen seasons old; you shall be black; your name shall be Tanga. Come Tanga, give me your hand, give it to me.'

'I'm frightened.'

'That word must die.'

'But . . .'

'Give me your hand and my story will be born in your veins. You'll see how, in my country, a child is born old since he cannot

7

carry the fragrance of springtime inside himself. How he has only his arms to give to the peanut fields.'

Her heart encased and with a tortured soul, Anna-Claude gives her her hand. The silence is so heavy that she hears an owl taking flight. She closes her eyes, having decided to let her terror recoil, to let herself be captivated. Beyond the locked away gaze, jumbled forms begin to rise, become sharper, sketching Tanga's life line by line, first a crack, then a notch, before she is entirely undressed. And Tanga's story flowed out into her until it became her own story.

◆

Before, I existed – I used to dream. I'd sink down underneath a mango tree for endless hours and run images through my mind. I was only ten but I was already imagining the man keeping an eye on my window, creating chances and coincidences so as to have the privilege of walking by my side. I waited; time kept passing. The dream did not materialise. I began to be bored.

Then the father old one died. And the mother old one had the idea to let me go on the road, to find other dreams. I tramped up and down the streets; I scoured the market-places. I no longer existed all by myself. Yet I was alone. Nothing but me. I brought my body to the crossroads of other lives. I put it underneath the light. A man approached me. I smiled. I followed. I undid my clothes. I placed my body on the bed, underneath his muscles. He snorted and shoved. Other images besieged me. I saw the man go back home at the break of day. Suddenly, at the threshold of his house, his pace slowed down. A moment of confusion. A flood of contradictory images. Public backsides – maternal breasts. A filthy room – family beds. A slimy mixture rejected by tradition, but oozing from the city's every pore. And I saw the man, still gorged with me, become entangled in lies so that the mystery remained of the mother-wife who, incorruptible, placed the birthday cake between her husband and me. I stopped the images, reality appeared, the man was still thrashing around. I felt nothing; I had no feelings, no sensations. Little by little my body had turned from flesh to stone, without my knowing it.

I remember the story of the man who led me to death. An ordinary day – the perpetual beginning, for we always have to begin again, begin all over again. That particular day, I saw him. The man, Hassan. Maybe it's sunny, maybe it's grey – I don't remember. One of those indefinable days on which the secret throbs of the city go unnoticed. I'm spinning round and round – like when I used to accompany the father old one to family reunions. Before we left the house he'd take me by the shoulders, and he'd always say: 'Don't forget, a child must keep its eyes lowered'. What I was left with were legs.

I'd follow him until we were under the storytelling tree and I'd sit down in a corner, on a bench. The adults would reminisce about earlier times in the village, talk of the evil-eyed chicken of cousin Bida, which had been stolen by the nephew of the brother-in-law of the cousin's husband. They'd curse those who mistreated tradition without being specific about their punishment. They preferred to leave the pains of determining the proper torture to the worn-out, deaf, and paralytic gods. They'd splutter. I wouldn't yawn. I was scrutinising legs, nothing but legs. Weak. Flabby. Shapeless. All of them revealed vices and shameful maladies.

The day I met Hassan, boredom and apathy were sitting by my side. He takes me by the hand, gives me a tour of the shops. I want to satisfy one of my passions: to contemplate legs, always looking at legs. The father old one said it; the father old one commanded it: 'A child must keep its eyes lowered.' And I always watched everything – just as much the advertisement showing a young woman in a mini-skirt, with her legs crossed, a cigarette in her smiling mouth, as the old lady wobbling on withered ankles and calloused feet through the vomit in the market-place. I watch, I'm strong, I am power. I can track a leg, an ankle, a foot without anyone's knowledge. I hunt them out, guided by admiration or pity – mostly by pity. They are my property. I dress them in a shroud, remove them from the world; with them I embark upon the retreat towards one's inner self, towards the darkness. My vision becomes blurred, my throat becomes a knot of sobs, I am inaugurating the ceremony of each dead day.

That day, I threw myself into the pursuit of my passion – those nervous skewers that pace the streets, move around, intertwine, disengage when pushed by inaudible desires. It matters little to me whether they are long, bony, short, fat. They are there, I am the other; I can see them, compare them, destroy them. They are there – my fleeing destiny suddenly has a meaning. With some cheating in my calculations, I'm finding myself taking stock of my life.

I met Hassan through his legs. I can see them still, grey trousers fitting them like a glove, crumpled around his penis and his belly. Black shoes. Yellow socks. They catch my eyes, attach strings to them forcing me to look at them, to look only at them from now on. Later and for days on end, to ward fate off, I wanted to forget, to assassinate desire. And sitting in front of a Coke with my head in my hands, I'd repeat: 'He's only looking to kill or exploit you.' I took a good look at the place of his seduction; I dug up the earth to kill it by its roots. It was pulverising me. I invited its reflections to attend the marriage of doubts. I found, wrapped up in my heart, the image of legs.

Hassan's legs. I see them parade before me. They move ahead, straight in my line of vision; they're laying the egg of desire in my body. Although the idea disgusts me, I know that these long legs which contract as he walks, despise women incapable of arousing groans of pleasure and hold the others in contempt. But legs like these, glued to our thighs, make the best lovers. They make us mad with tenderness and then, dead to all desire, they abandon us at dawn.

'How much?'

I raise my eyes. Before me stands arrogance itself. I classify it, put it where it belongs as does my mother old one and the mother of my mother old one before her. They always say, indeed they have always said: 'Disorder is the son of error.' So I label, I arrange the permitted norms and taboos in drawers. In my pupils I hold the arrogance of the man who has touched innumerable women. His wallet is heavy. His arched eyebrows strike up the hymn to greed. His fingers are long and slender. His eyes must contemplate his hands at length and pity them before he gets to work. Plastered down black hair. High forehead marked with pits. Undoubtedly smallpox. I detect his smile. Fleeting. Heavy. I understand that this meeting is going to turn me upside down.

Drawing out one's apathy is always a good thing. It leads us to action, even if every act is pointless – for example contributing one's belly to the ballet of bodies. Yes, loitering is useful, even if you become the shadow of a body submissive to loveable vices, because then at least you may end up serving some purpose, while you would have never served any purpose at all had you begun by thinking that loitering is useless.

◆

In the cell lit by a candle, the words suddenly dry up. Time stretches out: an impatient movement of Anna-Claude's. The dying woman opens eyes of anger.

'You think I'm cheating with my story, that since all physical sensations, all smells, have been eliminated, I'm wrapping it up in translucent paper just to embellish it. Don't deny it. Your hand has turned cold. It no longer transmits any warmth.'

'Don't be angry. I'm listening; I believe you.'

'Don't doubt me any more.'

'I promise.'

Anna-Claude squeezes the dying woman's hand very tightly. Sweat is beading on her forehead, trickling down her cheeks and her nose. She waits, with pinched mouth and nostrils, deaf to the cries and the laughter of the soldiers; she waits for the light that will brighten the semi-darkness of the soul. Hissing. Jingling. Shrieking. Nothing distracts her. She is there, her legs crossed, her head forward, her attention sharpened, ready to trifle with time, to recreate it so as not to panic at the approach of death. She wants to break through Tanga's mystery, the woman whose existence she knew nothing of, whom she would like to revive to shed light on life's shadows, in order to plumb the depths of her being. In the heavy silence within which she has decided to enclose herself, the words detach themselves once again from her body.

◆

11

At the words 'How much?', carelessly tossed out by Hassan, I feel my cheeks tingle. Shame grabs my heart. Rises in my throat, ties my head in knots. Until now I felt shame for only one thing, my mother old one. That shame is my breath which has no hope of survival. It persecutes me, chases after me, since the day that my mother old one laid me down underneath the banana tree so that I would be fulfilled at the hands of the clitoris snatcher. I can see her still, my mother old one, shimmering in her immaculate *kaba*, a black scarf in her hair, crying out to every god: 'She has become a woman, she has become a woman. With that,' as she taps her behind, 'she'll keep any man.' I didn't weep. I didn't say a thing. I fell heir to the blood between my legs. To a hole between my thighs. All that I was left with was the law of oblivion. Time passed, I was becoming accustomed to that part of me that was gone. I kidnapped the horde of memories. I tied them up with string. I shoved them deep inside the drawers of time. And here suddenly the horde re-emerged, in front of Hassan. It opened its drawers where watches were nestling, millions of watches, each one marking a different stage of my existence.

Hassan stands right in front of me. He is waiting, sure that he will submit me to his desire. The only two words he has spoken are enough to mark me, to take the husk off any amorous embrace in which I offer my body to feed the family. I refuse the costume which he wants me to put on my back. I'm suffocating in this fabric, cut by the echo into forever, a fabric drawn up on the balance-sheet by the blind accountant of the world, eager to file anything and everything. His fabric fits my body too closely. I need more fullness. I want to be different, I – the woman suckled in strength and character – I want to wake up in a clean and virgin skin. I want to persuade my demons to cut their tails and lower their horns, so that my angels can spread their wings. I want to paint the moment on the backdrop of what is coming, I who have no rights at all, I, obedience itself. I want to propel myself into the extraordinary: to be like everyone else. Aren't the streets elsewhere rich with the sighs of lovers, with the kernels of their laughter? I want to open up my body. I want everything that's possible in love to flow out into it. Sun! Trees! Palm trees! Where did they go, the potions that our grandmothers concocted to make love survive, despite morals that were wanting? I light the torches of my memory. They illuminate emptiness, nothing but emptiness. All I am left with is the lie with which to give birth to love. I survey its possibilities. A desire for perfection, for order. I stop time, I suspend the ladder of imagination, I clamber up, I change my clock, put a veil over my past. My voice rises, breaks. I split the word into pieces, I stretch it to the limit. I want to speak of renewal in this jumble where the dream awakens. I must salvage the precarious foundations of my reason. I plonk myself in front of him with my hands on my hips:

'I'm not a whore.'

Surprised, he remains speechless. I run towards the exit, the street that will carry me to myself. It's the hour at which night begins – agitated, crazy. Tropical night. Fast. Clean. Pitted with kerosene lamps and gaslights. Already the bodies available for pleasure, with daubed lips and waists cinched in *pagnes* or leather, are stationed on their own bit of pavement. Not far from them, men are wheeling about. Some are eating soybeans while making comments about the asses around the woodfires. Others just pass by. The street is spewing out its flow of cars. Horns are blowing. Brakes.

Hassan is following me. I turn around to make sure. I come near to him by keeping my distance. Something very new dwells inside me. I don't know its identity. Until now the only love that I, girlchild-woman, have had is hatred. A blind and ferocious hatred determined to destroy me with the force that belongs to feelings which know nothing other than the concern for a single being. It's impossible to share them. How do I explain to others that I hate myself? Some mornings, after spending a night negotiating with the night for sleep to gain the upper hand, twisting and turning in a soiled *pagne*, I pretend I have a migraine. I lock myself up in the shower room. I catch a glimpse in a mirror. I look. I look at myself until my vision is blurred. Flat nose. Heavy mouth. Pitiful breasts. I sprinkle myself with water, basins full of water to find again the virtues of the birth canal. Nothing changes, nothing must move. I was born from decay.

And here we are this evening, with my heart moving; Hassan is following me. I stop in front of a newsstand barely larger than a sentry box, lit by a candle. I leaf through a few newspapers several days old. In my country, the clock has stopped where culture begins . . . I look at them without seeing them, feeling them, drunk on the thought of living elsewhere, of dreaming elsewhere. The world is a stage. I am raising the dusty curtains of my life. I am becoming the independent, intellectual young woman, exasperated by the literary laxity of journalists. Being a so-called intellectual means looking embittered. Order, order once again, for one's place must be shifted without forgetting anything at all about oneself. And I, the girlchild-woman, I put on a slight squint just to make sure Hassan is my audience. He is right by my side, and crowding me to make a return to reality unbearable for me. He says that the 'free-thinking, free-flying woman', wearing *pagnes* that are easily tucked up, has stolen glory away from Woman. He says that my beauty is devouring his speech, for the word that rises from the lucid region of his thinking is muddied by imprecision and by the fragrance emanating from my body that has already begun to caress his skin. I become indignant, I detest that mixture of aggressiveness and indifference which absolute right confers. But I am pleased: he has let me know that something beautiful, perfected, has just started to exist within me. If I am not the spouse, if I come from farther away than she, I am managing to be her equal.

For I exist here in the eyes of the man, perched on his desire. Long before the sound itself, I know that what he'll say is:

'*I had settled in the ephemeral. Suddenly, there you are and I hear the crumpling of paper, the flight of the bee, the rustling of stars.*'

I am waiting; the words do not come. A few minutes of tangible silence. My look is questioning him, he opens his mouth, he doesn't mention love but proclaims that it will be a privilege to have a glass over which to make our acquaintance. I accept.

We sat down in the one elegant café in the town. A hushed atmosphere. Wall-to-wall carpeting. Club chairs. Broads at the bar, aseptic with their applied *ambi*, stinking in their *pagnes*. Men's eyes riveted on them, as vulgar as the flies of their jeans. A silence that speaks. A secret understanding between the bodies. A waiter comes by. Hassan orders two Cokes which we begin to sip.

'What's the matter? You're not talking,' I suddenly say to Hassan.

'I'm thinking.'

'What about?'

'About sex, about how to make love to you.'

'My genitals have been entombed underneath a banana tree for eight years.'

'I will exhume them. I'll polish them and take the years away. They will acquire the flush of their earliest beginning.'

'You all say the same thing.'

In the time that it takes for these words to sink in, Hassan rears up. I laugh to melt the tension. People are looking at me. My laughter breaks. I stick my face in my glass. He understands my embarrassment. His eyes become languid; he sing-songs: 'Love is blue'. His head bobs around, he lights a cigarette, smokes, coughs before taking control of his words. He doesn't speak of love but makes a plea for the pleasure his penis has exuded. He says: 'You'll be reborn underneath my muscles.' He talks to me about himself, his ambitions, his failures, beliefs he flees from but which pursue him.

'Yesterday morning, I found a dead bird on my desk . . . And one morning it was a shroud . . . On yet another morning, a colleague tried to bewitch me by stealing my handkerchief.'

Hassan. He belonged to that Africa that would marry without getting married, would divorce without divorcing, that domino Africa, its ass between two chairs, which would claim negritude on the one hand and pursue refrigerators and gas stoves on the other. He had let his hair grow long, rastafarian style, then he thought it was too long, too much like monkey turds. He'd straightened it. For the sake of African solidarity, he would invite people to the bar, poor people, kids off the street. He'd offer a round of drinks, he'd make small talk, they would thank him, and emotion would cut through him. High on his success, he'd swell up with pride, swell up in his office at the Postal Services where, surrounded by several ashtrays, he'd receive people and promise them jobs. He'd say: 'You'll have your job, but first you'll have to water the soil.' He'd hold out his hand for the banknote, people would rummage through their pockets, the job wouldn't appear, and still they'd continue to come in long lines, dragging their feet, trickling in, hope hanging on to their tail. They poured out endless flows of words which Hassan would be careful to redistribute equally among them all. They'd talk, sensibly or not and Hassan would listen to the words' vibrations, not understanding their meaning, not even trying to understand. He'd grasp states of mind, facts, he'd sigh, raise his hands to the sky in the face of this or that situation which he'd consider unfair, and he'd say that he wouldn't delay changing it in the manner of the gods themselves, this seeming only reasonable, and to which the spirits would agree. They'd continue to talk, be submissive, never catching their breath until they'd closed the doors behind them. Then he'd turn his air-conditioning on high to rid the room of their smell of old dirt and he'd light a cigarette.

Hassan. He was sincere in these procedures and this sincerity went perfectly with his inability to make anything materialise. He'd talk of leaving, of leaving by rarely used paths, by burying wives and children underneath the stone of oblivion. He said that such a break would bring him the new rain necessary to water other loves, other very young and very beautiful movements.

This particular day, he speaks to me and, as he sets out as an afterthought his ideal, his fantasy, blind to anything that isn't to do with himself, to anything that in outline already exists between us – the desire to speak overcomes me.

I would like to have said: I no longer feel like leaving to go anywhere, just like that; there is still too much emptiness that sounds beneath my steps. I would like to have told him: I want to exchange my dreams; I'd like to have a house with blue windows, a bed, the same man's voice to wake me every morning. I would like to have told him about the balcony; someone, always the same one, there in a dressing gown and slippers. I'd like to have spoken about the coffee, the cries of children, the dog, the magpie at the end of the meadow. I'd have liked to. I'd have liked to.

But words commit you. Words crystallise. And I, I've been a girlchild-woman from the start. A story that happens in a lifetime, every lifetime. No dreams, no memory, no illnesses. A thigh, breasts, buttocks. A mass of flesh poured out by the gods to announce the coming of woman, a swelling of flesh that will not be named.

I say nothing. I look at the man, the pile of words squeezed between his lips. I look and I picture his wrinkles ten years from now, his white hair, the rhythms that I won't be able to control, his follies, his bedazzlement. For me, the future is here and now. There's no question of staying behind! I have to move ahead, whatever the price, otherwise there is no story any more. With every minute, every second, every unwinding hour that goes by, drop by drop, I must keep this in my head: to be here, answering yes to my presence, standing straight in the sun and in the rain, in order to give the story its breath. Hassan is already getting up, pays the bill, and holds out his hand to me as he smiles.

Everything unfolds as it usually does with every other man. He whisks me off to one of those squalid rooms that share the peculiarity of always being the same – dirty walls. Posters. Newspapers. A low table. A leaking tap.

Without a word, I take off my raggedy clothes. He comes close to me, his eyes inspecting me. I am clothed in shame; I cover my breasts with my hands which he lifts off, smiling.

'I have love in my palms,' he says.

I don't respond; I'm looking at the wall, just the wall, wanting to take on its hardness. He understands my immobility, works around it as with an obstacle, picks up the track of speech to rid me of the mad weeds of anxiety.

'I like to see everything,' he says.

He shoves a hand in his pocket and takes out a scarf, hurling misgiving into my senses as he blindfolds me. Stripped down to my soul I wait, submissive to his desires. His voice rises, sometimes at my left ear, sometimes at my right, and I understand he's walking around me as children go around a Christmas tree. He says:

'Yes, you are a woman, you are grown up, slender despite your big ass. I'm crazy about you.'

I remain silent.

He says:

'You have green eyes, heavy breasts, your hair comes right down to your buttocks. That arouses me.'

I keep quiet. But I know, I the girlchild-woman, dutiful in the fulfilment of the rites of child-parent to her parents, since it's fitting that I sell my flesh to feed them, to feed them always because of the breath of life they gave me, I know that I am small and skinny, with short frizzy hair. But Hassan's words carry me off. Behind my blindfold, I close my eyes again, digging the abyss in which yesterday will be buried, in which the truths of a people ensnared in the

18

exploitation of children will be buried, while the rest of humanity radiantly dashes forward on to the path where the child is king. I'm dreaming of a gigantic setting where gestures create and caresses give birth to sensuality. I want to find woman again for want of the child.

Hassan takes me in his arms. Step by step, without letting go of me, he pushes me towards the bed. He collapses on top of my belly. 'Kiss me,' he demands. His lips subjugate me. He grabs one of my legs, then the other, puts them over his shoulders. He penetrates me. His steps cut through me. Woman's existence comes to me now. I hadn't known it, yet I recognise it. A memory engraved in the darkness of time. My body breaks loose, thumps, beats against the walls and partitions of my life. He soaks me. I push, it's new to me, I am transformed into an enormous wave.

I emerge from the wave of oblivion and from the moment of womanhood rediscovered by ripping my blindfold off: Hassan's eyes are tied up in a scarf. He doesn't hear me, fully concentrating on his pleasure. I put the blindfold back on.

Is it really necessary to fall into the deep waters of the invisible, to disappear in them, in order to reach the newly clad heavens? On this continent, where every truth is half empty or half full, what guile should one put on to have the full sun fall across one's body? Even happiness by proxy needs a face. I must get my own back again and mould myself into the state of being a woman forever, so that I will no longer be the child-parent of my parents.

It is ten o'clock. Hassan is getting dressed. Briskly he goes to the window, lifts a corner of the curtain and examines the night. I mimic his movement, allowing my body to get to know itself again. Nerves on edge are audible in my tone as I tell him: 'I'm leaving.' He suggests taking me home. I refuse. He insists. I hold fast to my refusal. He thinks that perhaps there is a father or a mother concerned about appearances. I don't enlighten him. How can I tell him that in my world both mother and father accept that he will besiege me and cause me to swell up as long as it brings material gain? How can I tell him about the bloody slashing of a mutilated childhood? My eyes upon the darkness, I tell myself that we are just two grains of sand carried in the hands of the wind. I could have

19

been blonde, dark, or a redhead. What difference does it make? In ten years, he may still be here with a girlchild-woman forgotten by the world – this world which holds itself together in the conviction that Africa's childhood is free, her savanna is nourishing. And he, he'll be here with this girlchild-woman, who's alive because she's breathing, dead since the stars were born.

Tears come to my eyes. I feel like crying about nothing, and I suddenly understand that until now, I've come upon stories that are all alike, stories that overlap, leaving not one trace of bitterness, but that today I want the episodes that come next, those that will set woman free and bury dead childhood forever. Like the others, those in far-off countries, I want to stride over unhappiness and step on board the train of my becoming.

◆

We separated on the corner of a street, with a kiss on the cheek and the promise to see each other tomorrow. Suddenly I'm rich, inhabited by the future. I've succeeded. From now on, I'll see happiness coming. It will breathe air into every nook and cranny of my life, just like the wind. Today. Tomorrow. The day after tomorrow. To love. To own. My mother old one always said to me: 'Your hands are like a sieve, my girl. Men run through your fingers like grains of sand.'

Today, I am woman. My mesh is growing tighter. I'll stop up my holes, every hole without a single mistake. I'll transform my lies into the truth. All I need to do is codify them, carve them out very carefully. That is how man has constructed his world, put together his history. From now on, I'll know what to do with my geography. Man will recognise me though I will have hardly been mentioned. I'll go to him, I'll hoist myself on top of a ladder to inscribe my soul into his desire. Then I'll pivot around myself. I'll take the spectacle of my past slough, slide towards it, lift up its *pagne*, rub its clitoris, set fire to pleasure, erase the flight of the black bird from my life, send my legs flying in the direction of the frontier; only then will I have access to the confiscated regions of happiness.

As I walk home, I come across unprotected girlchild-women offering their bodies. They're women or children, defined by mood or profit, sisters of a similar destiny, a similar despair, a mixed scent of girlchild-women who go through life without leaving any traces other than the ephemeral vibrations of a butterfly. Do they even breathe? Do they see death crawling up their body, tying it in a knot before abandoning it, stiff and cold, to the hands of some procurer of blood? All it takes is lifting their *pagnes* for their sexual organ to come into view with its throng of disguised hopes, losing its colour from one hour to the next, as it's transformed into an ossuary.

The hope of hope of hope! Not to be these women any more. Refuse the resemblance. Plough the paths of what's possible, of all possibilities. From now on, I'll arm myself against unhappiness. I'll put order into my own story, I'll give it the breath of amorous fables, I'll murder my monsters and I'll offer them in sacrifice to the heavenly powers. In order to escape from the reality, the miasmas inhaled at my mother old one's place, I'll enter the backwater of oblivion after having rid myself of my *pagnes*. I'll stay there for seven days and seven nights. Then I'll emerge from those purifying waters a virgin, and slowly I'll slide into the amnesia of the ordinary woman. Who is she? Will she be clothed in the love of a man who works during the day and comes home to her in the evening, while she, more woman than ever, places large, wonderfully smelling dishes on a damask tablecloth? These thoughts, unconnected to the joy living within me, irritate me.

I turn my head away from them – I don't want to hang on to reality; I want to do without it, if only for the here and now.

I'm doing my utmost to describe my heaven, for I, girlchild-woman, deprived of the sun, damned by men, I'm bringing myself back to the idea that from now on, I'll live 'something nobody will be able to take from me'. And I continue on my course, one-way, straight ahead. What I see are images of a world to come, a city furnished with my own inventions. Because from now on, I'll have little to do with these men who stroll in the streets, aroused only on a sexual level, different men all pulsing with the same behaviour, pierced by the same heat. The same pot of stew. As for me, I am elsewhere, absolutely centred.

I reach the front of the shanty where I live with my mother old one and my sister. Under the full moon, its sheet metal walls are shining like the anvil that shatters the iron block. It's been destroyed ten times. Ten times the mother old one has rebuilt it by hand, every willing hand in the neighbourhood. Every time the high and mighty come through, they tear us down, wrap us up, put us somewhere. 'The town must be kept clean,' they declare. And every time we rebuild again, with the patience of the poor in our fingers and our hearts full of hope that we'll be forgotten. Perhaps when they come through for the hundredth time, they'll open their eyes and take in the spectacle of our wretchedness? Then they'll notice that we are the shame that day in and day out they themselves have woven, under their egotistical leaders. Their canvas will shrink, we'll grow fatter. We'll invade air and space; they'll shake their jackets to hunt down the animal; they'll see us – we who are the fleas in their silk jackets; they'll see us put down our pestilential turds on the threshold of their dwellings.

◆

In the cell the air is oppressive. Mosquitoes are fluttering around on search patrol, exploding in a bouquet of blood on a cheek, a leg, an arm. Anna-Claude is becoming restless. One word, one more word, breathed by Tanga's body into her own flesh. She finds she is black, at the bend in a path, a sorrow, a death issued forth from ossified beliefs.

'Why are you questioning yourself?' Tanga suddenly says. 'You refuse to believe that I'm inhabiting you, and yet I am inside you.'

'I'm not denying a thing. You're speaking to me without opening your mouth, I can see that perfectly well. But I don't understand.'

'You have to believe with that faith in the obvious which is the naked truth, which is wisdom.'

'Nobody will believe me.'

'You'll tell my story ten times and nobody will believe you. You'll persist, and the eleventh time it will be fine. My story will be the bread dough that must be kneaded in order to survive. Let me free it up so as to build the future.'

Anna-Claude is silent and crosses her legs. She's a long way from using the kind of pseudo-intellectual speech in which terms ending

22

in *ism* are tossed about, all those chopping block terms that divide people and remove them from life: 'We must remain true to our convictions,' they splutter under their tattered flag, their eyes grim and hateful, their refrigerator stuffed with meats and delicacies. Elsewhere the earth is drying up inexorably.

Anna-Claude is concentrating. She wants to extract as much happiness as possible from these facts which gorged themselves on surliness. She wants life to be lived to the fullest, even if in the end there'll be hunger and thirst, even if she'll have to hold her nose because life will finally have a smell: the smell of death. Once again, words came to nourish the night.

◆

Mother old one is waiting for me, sitting on a mat, banknotes, collected and crinkled for months clutched in her fingers. Her grey *boubou* is worn underneath the armpits and around her shrivelled breasts. Her frizzy shock of hair, white in some places, has been gathered in two braids on top of her skull. The corners of her mouth, pulled down by all the setbacks, emphasise her woman's destiny which has emerged from nothingness and is going towards the void. Only money protects her from decay and holds death at bay. And always mother old one is one jump ahead with money, her haven. She counts it, she adds it up, and then the sun rises in her eyes. She becomes a child stuffed with candy, a man's penis buried deeply in the moist sludge of a woman. Emotions accumulate. Pleasure clambers up. And she hangs on to the money always – her lifebuoy. She is a step ahead of it just so that it won't pass her by. She isn't pushed by greed, mother old one. No. All that is there is the frantic desire to put a halt to the gusts of misfortune. She doesn't want to be like Mama Médé who, consumed by lack of money, had found her end open-mouthed in her hut, rotten all through, as smelly as a croaked dog. She doesn't want to end up like lady Dongué, the sorceress who'd been found with her nose in the mud, without any insides, without a heart, hacked to pieces by the *megang* she practised in order to amass wealth, always to amass wealth. Mother old one, she wanted to work her way around destiny.

My mother old one. She'd been born from a miracle. Her mother, Kadjaba Dongo, was an Essoko princess, short on brains, with firm high breasts, who used to get up at dawn. She'd offer her mouth and let out breathless laughter that would pull dozens of men along in the furrows of her skirts. She'd offer her rump to be kissed and pull it away before a move was made. They'd complain; she'd laugh, saying she'd give her body over to the caresses of the man who would commit the unknowable. They'd be unnerved; they were dreaming of collapsing in adoration. She'd raise the insurmountable obstacle of the extraordinary; they'd swear; she continued to unleash her requirements; their fury was increasing, reaching its apex. One day they decided that the time had come to destroy her, to bury her underneath live embers. They contrived strategies which brought them back to sit at her feet. On their own or in groups, talkative or silent with eyes lowered or raised, they asked what gesture was necessary to make her body open up to them. They lowered their trousers; some of them offered their bellies. Her hand would wander through the hair, and she'd catch hold of a member standing up straight as a spear, look them right in the eyes and feigning concern would say: 'But that one is going to rob me of my fertility.'

Time was dropping its beads through the hands of destiny. The strategy changed. One day while she was holding court, Kadjaba lay down on a mat underneath a mango tree. Maybe she was sleeping, maybe she was awake. They came alone or in groups. They spoke – she didn't answer, she didn't touch. They left. Then there was silence. She breathed deeply, ready to surrender herself to sleep when the last one came, veiled like a man of the desert. At last, something new! She didn't move, rigid with curiosity. He approached her, shored up her *pagne*, penetrated her roughly. Kadjaba arched up under the shock, bit her lips, then said: 'It's hot today.'

'Yes,' the rapist agreed, pulling her skirts back down.

She stood up to discover the body that had possessed her – and encountered two breasts, a vagina.

◆

24

During the days that followed, she took up the same position. Men came by, then a penis would arrive as unexpectedly as the last one – hot, pulsating with excitement. He'd take her and she'd feel the difference in size, length, but she didn't question it. He'd possess her until the day came when the strangest sounds went through her: 'Look at her,' people said, 'she's swallowed a coconut!'

A noise or an explosion? It mattered little. Mud and dirt were piled on Kadjaba, and began to form a hill which produced her future code of conduct. In the village where the commonplace was served for supper and slander for dessert, Kadjaba reinvented silence, casting the desperate sweetness of her desires to the wind. She no longer laughed. 'Only dogs bark,' she said. And she stopped lying in the sun so as not to have to hear any more.

One morning between two downpours during the rainy season, she felt the first pains of labour. Like a young wife, she put on her prettiest *pagne*, put up her braids and took the path to the banana grove. Time went by. Sweat. Pain. My mother old one was born. Kadjaba cut the umbilical cord, spat on the ground three times to put an end to her fertility. She swore that no child's cry would ever again come forth from her entrails and went home with my mother old one in her arms. She entrusted her to her mother.

This illegitimate birth poisoned Kadjaba's maternal instincts. It invaded her, stripped her of everything that wasn't herself, to the point where she stood in everlasting negation of others. She no longer washed, wore nothing but *pagnes* cut from floursacks, and military boots. And in order to break with everyone completely, she declared herself to be deaf and blind.

Mother old one, fed by her grandmother, chastised by her aunts under the sick eye of Kadjaba, grew up like a vagabond. No mat on which to put her grief to sleep. A lost sheep, absent and guilty of not having known how to share her mother's despair, she was eaten up by the feeling that this sadness, brought forth by her birth, would remain beyond her grasp forever. And she'd sing:

> *When mother was the water of the sea*
> *she's be ablaze in the evening*
> *she'd blaze in the blue foam of the sky*

25

where all the children of the universe
would shimmer like a thousand stars

When mother was the water of the sea
I used to go about the streets
to sing her memories
far away from the menacing ravens
and all around and everywhere
happiness would open its wings.

Out of spite towards herself, towards her body, she came to the conclusion that she'd bear hers – malevolent object – with eyes wide open so that troubles, mistakes, failures wouldn't encumber her path in the end.

At the dawn of her thirteenth year, she left and crossed the forest, found a palm tree that was losing its fruit. She took off her old rags and gathered up the nuts. She crouched down, spread her legs. She pushed every one of the nuts inside her vagina. She felt the burning, the scratching, still she continued. When she decided her cup was full, she ripped them out one by one. She was in pain, blood was dripping down her hands, her fingers. Tears were flowing, her nose was running. She said that pain was a condition in which to forget about the pleasure invented and constructed in bed. Mission accomplished? She rose, wiped herself with an end of her *pagne* and went back to the village. From that time on, she'd drag her body each day to the edge of the woods and catch grasshoppers which she pinned alive to a tree. She caught chicks, nailed them to a board and opened up their belly. She trapped rats, dropped them into boiling water and watching them struggle in the pot, she'd laugh, shrieking: 'There's the shelter, there's the shelter my mother wasn't able to find!'

Then my father appeared. She told herself it was time to chase away the curse, to stretch out between two rocks like a snake, to rub against them and leave her skin behind. It was time to change the register of her voice, to sing songs other than 'When mother was the water of the sea.'

From now on, she'd stay ahead of misfortune, she'd grip it with her claws, her teeth. She'd put it underneath a bale of straw, sprinkle it with petrol and burn it. She'd watch its wings take flight in smoke, then she would grow old clasped in the arms of happiness.

I have often thought of that encounter which sired me, that meeting that destroyed me and at the same time gave birth to me. That encounter which was to say to me later: since you're here, since you're alive, have a seat on the debris of the ages; feed us with your body. We no longer know, you'll know for us.

◆

Not everything went according to the way the old one had foreseen it. The eye of misfortune had been sculpted in marble between her thighs. She gave birth to me. My father cheated on her.

In the beginning they were escapades of an hour or two – he was doing the rounds of questionable beds where the power of money gave orders. My father old one loved women. Brunettes, blondes, redheads, black ones, but always woman – that ageless creature, well groomed, peeled down to her Venus de Milo. He loved that smell of rotten fish, those oozing breasts, those bellies that were wedded to desires without taking anything, those sloppy wombs whose waters had died. He loved them for the sickening things they contained, those public places, the dumping ground into which human excrement was emptied. He wallowed in them and waited with his tongue hanging out, panting. He waited until the smut was spewed back out, something which his ears no longer had the opportunity to enjoy since he had married my mother old one. He heard them, with their drawn faces, their loins harpooned and their eyes closed to this one-sided marriage. And very quickly the requirements of his fantasies changed into an obsession. From there on he needed more than one closely timed escapade to satisfy himself.

Some nights, when reluctant sleep keeps its distance, I see the phantoms emerge, dragging me into their paralysis. I fight back. I shout. They follow me, persecute me, collide with me. I call my father, I call my mother. They don't hear me. I scream louder. Monsters congregate around me. Two vultures where the eyes should be. Horns where the nails should be. They penetrate me, they lacerate me. I see my entrails in their hands. They laugh through the gaping holes of their missing teeth. They string my intestines on to amulets and hang them around the neck of my parents. I close my eyes; I want them to leave me alone. I want to bury my bitterness in the slimy earth, to hold on to the idea of the marriage I had created for myself. I want to invent the three dreams that diminish human suffering. I want to exist differently. I want to go through the streets, take up my position in a corner and disembowel a man. They'll come to arrest me, to interrogate me. They'll listen to my voice, take notes. I shall reply; I shall speak about the children separated from life, locked up in the cage of death. I shall speak about those who drink large cups of sadness. But who will believe me? The world prefers the silence that covers up the thorn.

I am a child. I do not exist. My age cancels me out. My heart lies rooted in a forest of sand.

Is it a dream that assails me today or is it a memory? It was a Wednesday – my birthday. Father had been gone well beyond the usual limits. The food, a *maffé*, was getting cold. Evening had fallen. It was bolting up the entrance, covering up the windows. My mother lit the lamp. He was bound to come at the end of the darkness. Priority of priorities. From time to time, she took a quick look at the clock. Nine o'clock. Midnight. Man, where are you? On to what gravestone have you crashed down? Worry cut itself into her face, twisting her mouth. She paced the room; her feet cracked. I was watching her with my heart swaddled in pity. I saw this woman, my mother, the shadow of a being who didn't know herself, evolve during this absence. I was observing her, I was becoming an adult. I was growing up, I was growing old, my teeth were falling out, my skin was withering. I became tall, I looked at the road, every road of love, and I placed myself inside the point at which I would be invisible. I became air, I mixed with it. Not the hot and humid air of my country. But air that was cold, the air of exile. Flee. Flee. Flee.

The old man came back at dawn with lowered eyes. His clothes were crumpled in the area round his penis and his belly. As soon as the old woman saw him, she rooted herself in front of him, feet solidly on the ground, her hands on her hips.

'So where were you, eh?'

'Let me get by, please. We'll talk later. I'm a wreck.'

Where have you come from? I have to know. You're dishonouring me in front of my children – in front of the whole world. You can't even manage to spend a single day with your family to celebrate your daughter's birthday. You have no respect for anything; nothing stops you.'

'Listen . . .'

'No!'

She raised her hand; he grabbed her wrists and pushed her firmly on to the mat.

'Let's put our cards on the table,' my father hammers on. 'Is that what you want then?'

There was a silence. Not one of those flat silences that offers a haven of peace after a hurricane, but a silence riddled with grief and hate. Father old one exploded. He said that mother old one's sex had set before the sun and that she ought to let the goat graze where the grass grows. Mother old one remained silent. He told her she had ruined him. She had stolen his oxygen pump, and that from now on he'd get himself dirty in other women's asses in order to survive. Mother old one remained silent. He told her that down there – in the place between someone's legs where he unburdens his loins – woman had a sickening smell but one that pleased him, for on her head the long braid of hope sat enthroned. Mother old one remained silent. Father old one went on, insulting her, justifying himself. I was listening to him; I heard him; I understood nothing; I saw. I heard him erect the scaffolding of his life, planning it in such a way as to afford himself an unlimited number of these shameful weddings in which the man gathers the honey of every flower within the reach of his genitals. I heard him legitimise these relationships, lay down the law, establish a new civil code. The one that was soon to rule our house. And mother old one, looking like a retarded child, was listening, curled up on her mat, without any sign of rebellion. My father fell silent. She got up, went over to him, stuck a finger down her throat and puked before bursting into laughter. She laughed and said that man has sinned against woman and that his punishment should equal the extent of his error. She said that the ancestors would come down from their trees to wash the error away, but that a new brand of detergent would be needed, and ancestors other than those of the collective memory . . . She spoke, hiccuped, and laughed. The old man, not knowing what to do, began to laugh as well. He understood this laughter was directed at him, against his dignity as a man. He knew he had to react, to reestablish order. But he was laughing. He was laughing and shrieking in turn, yelling a series of incomprehensible sentences, a long string of words. Eve had led man to sin. My mother had driven him to madness.

Standing on the ashes of my dreams, I was watching night fall. Eight and four make one, eight and four make one. Time, which until now I had thought to be indestructible, was disintegrating. My destiny was swaying to and fro. Anguish was seething. The days had ceased to fall in line with the sun. I had never been born; I had been born since forever. I had always known or never known these mad people. I had seen this table, this sister of mine, this alarm clock, on the planet Mars or Jupiter. What difference did it make? I was going crazy myself. They didn't see it, they didn't hear it. I was going mad. I had to sleep. To sleep inside the folds of my night. My parents had devoured my life, driven nails into its shroud. I had to draw the curtain over ugliness. I slept for five days and five nights. I was waiting for time. I wanted it to track down my lice and my spiders. To let it undo the long braid of despair. In vain. At dawn on the sixth day I left my room; I left my body to retouch life. It kept escaping me, and nobody saw it.

And so it was that the man my father who, not content to bring his mistresses home, to fiddle with them under my mother's disgusted gaze, would later rip me apart in the budding of my twelfth year. And so it was that this man my father – who made me pregnant and poisoned the child, our child, his grandson – this man never noticed my suffering, and yet it lasted until the day he died, until the day of my own death.

And so it was, too, that the woman my mother, who was to accept these women invading her bed, welcomed them and wove the presence of the rejected wife around them. This woman my mother, who coughed discreetly into her skirts when she saw me give birth to the child her man had sired; the woman my mother, who hated her man without a gesture, and who, to avert malediction and shame, hoodwinked everybody with the eternal tale of the child that had come from lord knows where and of the depraved girl; this woman, my mother, didn't see the tree plunged in mourning that I had become, the tree standing in the night. She no longer heard – the woman my mother was asleep.

And so too, it was that my sister, little girl of burdensome virtue, who hid behind her candid looks in order not to understand or see; so too, my sister, the exact copy of my mother, as beautiful and as cowardly as she; so it was that my sister, hiding behind the veil of fear, smiled her ignorance as she saw my belly grow, grow to the height of my soul and she said: 'Isn't it true, Big One, that babies are found in cabbage patches?'

In the cell, the air is a prison. Walls and women, closely connected, deliver themselves to the world's enigmas – its secret actions. Here the whys, constructed under cruelty's aegis, no longer have an answer and even evidence, tightly packed inside the brain, questions itself. Why? Why what? Useless questions pushing them towards an encounter with the void, binding them to the work of death.

To survive, to survive! Anna-Claude keeps repeating it to herself. She must still learn how to see without looking, how to understand from the heart. During the interrogation Anna-Claude, alone and anxious, keeps the questions where they belong – in her head.

'How is it possible?'

'Be quiet,' replies Tanga. 'White people are born in pink ribbons. As for us, we're born on piles of rubble.'

'You aren't born black, you become black.'

'You know nothing about suffering.'

'Yes, I do. I know that I know.'

'How could you? It has never knocked on your door.'

'You're wrong. Death is even closer to the living than to the dying.'

'It's not eating away at you.'

'Oh yes, it is! I hear your night as I hear death ululating. I hear the screeching of everything that crawls, slithers, and chills the spine. It does no good to plug up my ears, ball my fists, close my eyes – I still see the rumbling belly of the night come near. I am Tanga; I don't need to console you. I hear you, woman, even if understanding sometimes escapes me. If I didn't know suffering, do you think you'd be able to pour out the chaos of your landscape into my heart? I will dance on top of these unspeakable things so as to bury the pink rose of yesteryear inside your spirit. For I know, woman, I know the time has come; the time that attacks, dries out, and withers the flower in full bloom.'

'Stop your raving or I won't talk.'

32

'I'm not raving, woman. I'm telling your tale, to perpetuate your life.'

'You're interrupting me.'

'Speak.'

'You're not listening to me.'

'Yes, I am. You were talking about your grandmother, your mother. And now you have to tell me how she reacted when you came home after your meeting with Hassan.'

A grimace deforms the lips of the dying woman. Her eyes stare at the wall. She's watching for the monsters of madness. Anna-Claude takes her hand again, which had slid alongside her body – a hand stiff with tension which exhausts her. A few minutes pass, bringing the tiniest vibration that sets the story in motion again. And once again, the two women were joined together.

◆

My mother old one looks at me with eyes filled with hostile silence and she riddles my forehead with black holes. I turn my head away. The rank smell of one of those crises which explodes regularly since the death of my father old one, floats through the room. I smell it, I see it. They blow up in the least obvious places before they shatter the heart. Mother old one always chooses those moments when I am happy without her, when I withdraw into myself to give my body some rest. When I say to her: 'Ma, it is time for me to look after myself', whatever the place – be it the kitchen or the living-room – the face of mother old one changes and turns. Her eyes pop out. Her body becomes a suffering wreck. She lets herself slide down on the ground and writhes, with foam coming from the corners of her mouth. She says she is ill, that she's going to die; she puts a hand on her thigh, her arm and finally on her heart. My sister rushes over and gives her a glass of water. She drinks, she hiccups, she forgets what she's saying, her ideas. My sister drags her to her room, on to her bed. She lets herself sink down. For several days she lets herself go. She no longer moves, she no longer eats, she loses weight. I call in the healer. He prescribes potions which mother old one refuses to take. She says she's waiting for death and that it's slow in coming and that her wait is a long one. I am worried; I go back on the street and slip my body into caresses. I go to the market-place, I choose a *pagne* – a very brightly coloured Wax – and take it to her room. I open the curtains, she turns around covering her eyes. I walk around the bed to her side and kneel down:

'Look what I brought you,' I say as I rustle the fabric. She opens her eyes. Her lips open wide.

'Maybe I'd better wait for death standing up.'

She looks as if she's going to rise. I stop her movement.

'You're still too weak.'

'I can sit down.'

'Not until you've had a solid meal.'

I go to the kitchen and get to work. An hour later I come back with a plate of steaming *pépé* soup in my hands. I put several pillows behind her back for support and I feed her. She swallows a few spoonfuls, makes a face and shakes her head. I persist. She refuses. I insist and become more and more tense because I'm afraid she's waiting for death again. I say: 'Ma, wait for me, I'll be right back.' I rush into the kitchen. I come back with a basin of water and a towel. I wash her, I massage her until I have no feeling left in my fingers. I like the cracking of her bones underneath her old, withered skin. Then I wipe her dry and put colour on her nails, her eyelids, her lips. I back away to check my work of art. Proud? I pick up the new *pagne* and put it over her shoulders. I hand her a mirror. She refuses to look, saying:

'I am ugly. If your father saw me now . . .'

'Pa is dead.'

'Thank God I've known a few other moons since he's gone.'

'You deserve that, Ma.'

She'd smile, she'd weep, things would fall back into place. I'd lose my life, I'd sink into despair. At night, alone with myself, alone robed in my anguish, I'd write a letter to a man I didn't know.

Sir,
Your smell assails and sickens me. You have no words of love.
Yet I wish to be loved by you, by him, or by someone else. You
give me your penis. Cries come out of my mouth while my

34

womb is silent. I receive your ocean and interpret my wounds. How, sir, can I tell you of the sadness of a garden without any flowers? You pay in cash. You turn your eyes away. You go back out into the street with the smell of my sex in your nostrils.

Thank you, sir!

But that particular evening, after the meeting with Hassan, the world turned upside down and I no longer want to write any letters. Man is in my loins, in my breasts, on my lips. He is extricating me from my role as the child-parent to her parents. This evening I want to put them all to sleep forever – mother old one, unhappiness, everything together – so I can be as happy as I wish to be. To eat and drink happiness. I throw a glance at the ceiling. Rats and cockroaches are parading their disgust. As used to them as some people are to their dogs or cats, we no longer bother to crush or kill them. When they take us for hilltops and climb over us, we brush them away with our hands as others might do to a breadcrumb at the corner of their mouths. Sometimes a smell of decay announces the time for mourning. We ferret around, comb the place – underneath the beds, between the furniture. We discover a dead rat. We escort it to the cemetery behind the house. We cover it over with dirt and forget about it.

This evening, it's mother old one whom I want to prohibit from lodging in my memory. I look at the kerosene lamp on the table, the walls of sheet metal and the boards; the stove, the formica cabinet lined with thick beige veins, the wicker furniture – all the objects piled on top of mother old one's cart, my mother, whose avalanche of gestures racks my childhood. I say my farewells to them; there's nothing left to say to them. I've decided to live, I've nothing to do with mother old one any longer. She pasted so much sludge on to my birth that all the tidewaters on earth couldn't wash it away: in her mission as mother, she removed the bird from its nest. I take God as my witness. I told him that on my continent – my body – he has granted only a sun without light, only the sun's burning without its red blaze. My childhood is populated with bats, black birds and woodlice. My town stinks, my body has never felt a thing. Too many clouds drift by, higher than the stairway of the sky, smeared with suffering. I demand a day, one single day of light to disinfect the whole bloody mess.

I make a motion of going towards my room where I'll find myself again. The old one upbraids me. Had she picked up the waves of my metamorphosis? I couldn't say. Antagonised, I turn around, ready to invite her to warfare.

'Where have you been, looking like that?'

'Out.'

'Did you bring anything back?'

'Not a thing.'

'Some days are better than others.'

'There won't be any tomorrow. I'm stopping.'

'Is Monsieur John going to marry you?'

'No, he isn't, neither is anyone else. I'm finishing, full stop.'

Silence falls. The old one looks at me without daring to say what she senses, what she understands. But I, girlchild-woman, I know she's afraid this means being permanently abandoned. She's there before me, stripped of the mother's gestures, stripped of the woman's gestures, with nothing but trouble and fear to come.

And I, girlchild-woman, I take advantage of her loss to ponder over Monsieur John. I've never been able to call him anything but Monsieur John. There are those who're born with the title 'Monsieur' glued to their ass. He is one of them. And when I want to conquer the world like God, I add 'dear friend' to it which whips his desire into a frenzy and makes him kneel at my feet. He is an arms dealer, he's killed fourteen people, wears a big diamond on his ring-finger, and uses vanilla perfume. With his friends he discusses the stockmarket or his sexual prowess. In private, he knits sweaters for me and coddles me. He is cut out to be the one to pay, to open car doors, to offer compliments. I met him one afternoon. The sun is a quarter of the way down. A hypnotic sky. I'm hot. I'm bored underneath the corrugated sheet metal. I throw on a dress and a fake fur coat. I take the rue du Maréchal-Kany. I want to find some enchantment – some consolation – in the admiring looks that will be captured by my charms. I move ahead in a sweat on the look-out for rolling eyes and the comments of the envious horde: 'Hey! How much did that gear cost?' 'Pretty fancy, all that!' 'Ay! Aids! Aids!'

'Nah, the clap – only the clap,' 'Eh, eh, me, I wouldn't mind that poison in my bed.'

A Mercedes-Benz slides by next to me. Gleaming. An air-conditioned black guy. His mug a malaria-grey. Eyes the same. Dentures. Pays well. I close my critical eye. I direct the other one on the Benz, the diamond, the Rollex and all that they imply in terms of presents. These marvels come from a harmony sent by God – the heavens – to cleanse filth, to reinvent beauty. They fit my personality. If I wasn't born to set the world on fire, I can at least let its glare blind me. I climb into the car.

Monsieur John takes me to a hotel room. He gets undressed. He describes every one of my poses, every one of my shapes, even what's invisible. Then he recites the music of his life to me: 'Once upon a time, in a silver and golden forest, a valiant prince who couldn't find a woman to match him for brilliance of mind and soul . . .' The more he holds forth, the more I calm down. I'm looking through his eyes. I see the palace, the silver and gilded crockery, the crystal chandeliers, and the golden carriage. And so, steeped in illusions, I let the indulgence of my imagination turn me upside down. After two or three thrusts, a groaning in his throat, he collapsed on top of me and fell asleep. 'Next time,' he'll say when he wakes up, 'it will be better.' He'd wrapped me in swaddling clothes.

Thinking about him that evening, I get cramps in my belly, nausea grabs my heart. Vomit! Vomit! Vomit! Monsieur John. A clammy body. Putrefaction. A clump in a mouth that's devoured it all – sweet things as well as bitter. You have to let it go or it will rot your palate. Slowly, I turn my head towards mother old one with all the violent force now inside me.

'Don't count on me to see that horror again.'

'Ugliness is not something contagious, my girl.'

'So you take him on. If he wants you, that is.'

'When I was young . . .', she begins and lowers her head.

I know – I, her child who knows her better than she does herself – I know that her scrawny body is going towards an encounter with tears in order to drown out my desires. I watch her sow the seeds of blackmail and water them. It's growing all around me, forming a hedge to imprison me inside her garden of brambles. But as for me,

37

tonight I have decided to live. I fight back. I rend the heavens so as to destroy unhappiness. From now on, I'll put myself before everything. Before the world, Me; after the world, Me; always Me. I've decided to contemplate my navel as long as possible, right up to the limit, go beyond it and come back to my navel. Mother old one doesn't look at it with the same eye. She rises. She pulls at her *pagne* which falls like a rag around her ankles. She steps across it. She plonks herself in front of me. She looks at me vacantly, then begins to pace the room shaking her behind. She stops. She's breathing hard. She girates her pelvis. Obscene movements. I take refuge elsewhere. The absurd is tying knots in my gut. It's the same old story inside my head. Mother old one lifts up a leg, then the other and claps her hands. What's come over her? What is coming over her? She's dancing and me, I'm watching. I watch the woman forget what she used to be before. I know she's following the motions of death. I watch – is that not what the role of a child should be? How much time went by? I couldn't say. Exhausted, she stops dancing. Dripping wet. Her arms fall. She drops into a chair, puts her wrinkled face in her hands and weeps. I go over to her, enclose her in my arms, but her grief refuses love and offers only violence.

'Get the hell out! Ungrateful wretch! I don't want to see any more of you . . .'

'But . . .'

'Get the hell out! Bitch! You want me dead . . . But you'll go before I do. Day and night I'm going to be praying to heaven. It will fill your vagina with stones. And the words I speak today will come true, as true as the fact that I carried you in my belly for nine moons.' She spits on the ground three times, claps her hands so that the night of owls will carry her voice way beyond the treetops and the waters.

My life is a deconsecrated room. Terror and sorrow rip me apart. There are no emotions left to betray. I let my body manage itself. I hum a popular song. I try to empty the painful gourd of being cursed. To flee. Flee. Flee. I love flight. I love my body in flight. At moments like this I no longer really know whether I am crazy or simply a stranger to myself. I love these moments where I leave without having packed my bags or bought a ticket. I no longer

38

become entangled in the array of colours; the body no longer exalts me. Only the spirit counts. To be spirit only – to watch the world, to bear witness, to keep my steps steady. I love these moments when I can bend over the child I could have been, bring solace to her troubles with my breath. Only then am I able to take death in my arms and give her the warmth of death.

Mother old one is getting upset. Stinking words come tumbling out from the depths of her throat. She fiddles with her breasts. A few drops of milk spurt out and fall at my feet. I bend down to gather up the fruit of the woman's breasts, in order to discover the surprises and the miracles of childhood. I lick my fingers. A kick in the ribs sends me crashing to the floor. It's mother old one. With her hands on her head, she shrieks:

'Witch! You dirty witch! You want to get back into my belly feet first! Help! She wants to kill me. My God . . . My God.' She screams, punctuating every word with a kick.

And I, girlchild-woman, who wanted to go back to the land where parents are innocent of every crime, a world that's whole and matches my desires, I set my body in motion looking for the path of unreality so I won't have to describe to pain and affliction the harshness of its slopes. The idea comes to me of painting mother old one with whimsical visions. She can holler; I've already packed my bags.

In the savanna, a little girl milks a cow.

In the street, on the threshold of prostitution, two gigantic breasts hang down from the sky.

A sow-woman, her rump in the air, rolls her eighteen nipples in the mud.

Not one tear leaves my eyes to fall on the burns caused by her kicks. I'm getting in the mood to laugh. The room is filling up with a swell of feelings and thoughts. My heart is beating hard. My spirit becomes activated. I'm deconstructing my mother! It's an act of birth. It's madness to believe that the blood bond is indestructible! Foolishness to think that the act of existing within a clan implies guaranteed quality! Let's question the post to which we moor our boat! We're breaking nothing since nothing exists; since it is ours endlessly to invent the circuit.

As my reflections continue, so my universe widens, pushed on by

39

the wind of the spirit. In advance I foreswear anything, shadow or light, that will explode this situation. Perhaps God reigns over the universe, but as for me, I annihilate the world at my feet, since my state causes the world in which blood bonds exist to overturn, and a world in which they don't exist to emerge. If someone had taken a photograph of me, some other face, some other woman would have emerged. A woman who was pure, wise, and as clamorous as death. I am the custodian of a particle of light, of a fragment of joy hidden underneath my clothes. Like time, like the oracle, I am motionless despite mother old one's wish to impose guidelines upon me so as to devour me better.

I escape from her, I dispose of her. Go to hell, Ma! I am becoming a tower. I have clearly demarcated borders. From now on, you'll need a key to penetrate me. Mother old one doesn't know this secret. In order to break through it, she'll need to kneel down before me – only then will she become aware of what I know.

Little by little, the old woman calms down. And being so close to restored calm makes her resemble the young girl she once was, when she dragged a burdensome virginity around as her capital, sealed between her legs. Without taking her eyes off me, slowly, very slowly, she sits down again, looks around anxiously like someone who's lost and begins to think he's made an error and has no business being there.

'I curse you,' she says to me in a hoarse voice. 'You'll die in shit and piss. I curse you . . . And these words I speak today will come true – as true as the fact that I carried you in my belly for nine moons.' She spits on the ground three times, claps her hands. I felt the curse fire into my guts.

◆

'You should have left that night,' says Anna-Claude, interrupting the flow of the dialogue. Tanga looks at her. Eyes staring and open wide. Lips cracked. She is gripped by such ingenuousness. She nestles her hand more deeply in the other one's and says in a voice worn out with suffering:

'I couldn't have done it, woman.'

40

'You are strong; you could have done it.'

'No.'

'And why not? It was the opportunity to start from scratch, to build a new life.'

'Impossible. In my country, the child is born an adult, responsible for its parents.'

'That's not normal. It's a country of madmen!'

'Here, even God is mad. He's painted the world in a whirl.'

Anna-Claude, sobs stuck in her throat, lets her body curve around itself, like a shrimp.

'I'd like to smoke a cigarette.'

'Close your eyes and you can smoke as many cigarettes as your heart desires.'

'Go to hell. Dreams! dreams! I'm sick of escaping from reality. That's all I've ever done all my life. Escape from rejection, hatred, the hard luck of the Jews. I want real cigarettes, and to smoke until my eyes begin to water. D'you understand?'

Tanga's face assumes that rigidity that belongs to someone who refuses to put up with a whim but has only his eyes with which to express the outburst of his anger. The change escapes Anna-Claude. She rises, goes towards the door, tries to find whatever free space there is as she puts her eye to the keyhole. With some acrobatic contorsions, she can distinguish bars and some human wrecks on the other side of a narrow hallway. Some of the wrecks are huddled up around themselves, others are chained together. The idea that she resembles them crosses her mind, disorientated as she is by her days in prison. The claw of anguish settles into her flesh and rips it apart. She drums on the door, and yells: 'I want to get out! Let me leave! I've done nothing wrong. I haven't done anything.'

Sounds of footsteps. A soldier appears. A khaki shirt unbuttoned over a belly studded with small twists of hair. He has the rough and dull-witted look of one who works for the devil. He stretches, yawns and looks at Anna-Claude with a gaze full of contempt. 'What's she want, that one there, eh?' And without giving her time to answer, he yells to his comrades dozing over their submachine guns: 'Look at these sluts will you, they woke me up! Ah the whores! If it were up

41

to me, they'd be thrown in the sea, and God knows there's enough sea for all of them.'

Sleepy voices are heard: 'Break her bones', 'Why not fuck her instead and leave us alone', 'Shit! we want to get some sleep.'

The soldier puffs up his cheeks: 'So tell me – and hurry it up – why did you wake me?'

Anna-Claude casts a bewildered look towards the wall. She'd like to see her arms transformed into butterfly wings – to flutter through space in order not to have to reply to this murderous face who's reciting his miserable speech. She'd like to open her arms so wide that in the agony of their stretch she could find the excuse to dread freedom, she'd like . . . But anger already fills the soldier and makes him speak again.

'So, what d'you want, eh?'

'A cigarette, please.'

'A cigarette, please,' he mimics her. 'Why not caviar? D'you think you're in Europe, bitch?'

The insult galvanises Anna-Claude.

'No, chief. I think I'm on mankind's earth,' she says as she points her finger to the ground. 'And you, you are slaughtering this earth.'

The soldier lets rage entrench itself, take root in him, so that its flowers gorged on venom bloom in a loud crackling discharge. He yells and shrieks obscenities with foam on his lips. He says he'll corrode her loins with his saliva – that's all she deserves, to be reduced to the purest excrement. He says that he'll adjust the hatches to her size and lock her up in her own shit. He says that finally, when every fly in the world will have caressed her, he'll lean over her, his prisoner, and dance the hideous round of death.

Anna-Claude hears the words without feeling them, words enveloped in bark as if they were meant for someone else. Her wings are sprouting and place her in the realm of the extraordinary – in the dream. The soldier knows this and the silence that flows out from the woman causes his rage to escalate. He hits her. He tears her dress. He leaves her naked to the world, naked to him, and orders her to run around the room, clothed only in her skin. She tries to hide her triangle of love. 'No way!' he thunders. 'Hands behind your neck.' She submits and she turns round in circles – the question of love in the shadows, and nothing but vertigo which carries and sustains her – until the moment when the words escape from her mouth by themselves: 'Please chief, please chief.' Her footsteps want to stop in their tracks. The soldier gives her a kick. Her feet set off again. Other soldiers come running in, stinking of wine, garlic and violence. Like scattered gunfire, curses rise and go up to heaven before they crash down on the woman. Laughter. Beatings.

'Perhaps we can cut her clitoris off,' one of them suggests with a stutter.

'That would be too much of an honour for her,' another retorts.

'Me, I know what she deserves,' a third one says with a mysterious look on his face. 'We're going to offer her a cigar.'

And without any further ado, he lowers his pants and shits. Laughter. Cheers. The door is closed again.

It isn't life in the cell. Nor yet the void. Lizards climb the walls, their steps mingling with graffiti, there for eternity. Names. A date. A heart pierced by an arrow. Cockroaches. Rats. Fleas. They're all there; they are there – two women united in the suffering of these moments that follow each other but never become a length of time. Spirits of women who no longer obey the cycle of sun and night. Are they indifferent? They need to transform the body into a machine, so that hatred and violence will not become their inheritance.

Tanga, her gaze a sheaf of fire, sees shivers of shame run through Anna-Claude's body. In the space of a few seconds, her flesh tightens up again, rediscovering the dark and universal infinity where death and its monotony live. She tells herself that the world is a jungle in which man hunts man; that history is a meaningless suicide and that violence is merely a response – a clean and precise response, a response without the digression that would give it its definition. These thoughts exhaust her. She coughs, her lungs tight from the stale air in the room. She raises one hand and signals Anna-Claude to come closer, to get away from the foul corner the soldiers have left behind. Slowly, the woman releases her body which is tight with pain, crosses the space that separates them and lies down close to the dying woman. Even though weapons failed her, she knows the hour has come to entertain some hope, to lock away the flood of aggression in the cavern of the mad in order to think up some human wishes.

'You are right, woman. We mustn't stray from the dream.'

'You do understand then, though none too soon!' the dying woman jokes.

'Yes, we must live the dream. Tonight, you'll be Ousmane, my dream.'

'I shall give you fertility.'

44

'I shall give myself to you.'

'I'll make you some kids to perpetuate other kinds of human beings.'

'Love me.'

Their bodies intertwine. Anna-Claude weeps. Tanga traces grooves of tenderness on her neck and her loins. She tells her not to cry, that they have only just become acquainted with the nightmare, but that the embrace is the reality. She tells her that they will stroke their despair and that the most maternal of all love will gush forth from them. She tells her to dry her tears, so that the scab will fall off the wound of unhappiness. She cradles her, cajoles her, tells her that it's time to continue her story before time begins to celebrate the ceremony of her death. She adds: 'Don't forget, woman, you must know the rest of my life before you can perpetuate it.' The sobs begin to fade. Anna-Claude is calming down. Love's hands sweep away the poisoned remnants of pain, every trace left by its calloused steps. She blows her nose noisily and causes the wind of hope to rise as she curls more closely against Tanga. And once again, the words follow one another from the body of nascent death to her body, resuscitating a vanished childhood.

◆

In my room, I find peace again. I snuggle close to my sister. She's snoring. I guess at her face and her flat shapes in the darkness. They fill my eyes. She sleeps as I do – as everyone does – without any peculiarity. A pity! Something like an identifying mark should set happy people apart from the others.

I enter her body through the recesses of her armpits and her thighs. I take in her scents of oysters and dew. The night's silence makes me feverish. I go back to the noises of the day. Between crying and laughter, I see Hassan again. He acquaints himself with me in order to better establish his presence – so that I'll no longer know how to live without him. I can guess where he is pulling me. Confronted with life, this man will not look at me; he won't speak to me – he will possess me. And I will stay there; I will wait for him, because I am a girlchild-woman and not the first one in his damnable

45

life. At this thought a dull pain is distilled inside me – that unbearable pain known only by those who love unconditionally and who feel they're being devoured without receiving any nourishment in return. And, because I am a girlchild-woman, and not the first one to occupy his bed, a girlchild-woman without rank or classification, and because I am one of those whom he swallows and expels, I know it is appropriate to be a woman in order to capture his love. From now on, I will be so. I will be the woman dressed in white, a garland of flowers in my hair to weave life tirelessly, so that each day will be life. I will have my house, the garden, the dog, the magpie at the end of the meadow, children. The last word pulls me up short. Children, real ones, not this childhood of Iningué where the child does not exist, has no identity . . . Has parents to provide for and gets beaten so it will obey.

So it is for Mouélé's daughter, sold into prostitution.

So it is for Dakassi's son, who sells peanuts.

So it is for Tchoumbi's son, the child whose hands are cracked open all the way to his wrists. He says it's because of the weight of the suitcases and bags. Every day, both in the dry and the rainy season, he gets up from his straw mat before dawn appears, torso and feet bare, his little red shorts shrivelled up with filth and tight in the crack between his buttocks. He goes towards the station, the market-place, wherever suffering is carted around on the backs of men. Sometimes at high noon, at the hour when chickens and dogs seek out the shadow of the mango trees, at the hour when the 'air-conditioned blacks' hurriedly raise the windows of their frozen cars, you can see him – you'll recognise him. He moves ahead slowly, huddled underneath a sack of millet or corn, quite disposed to dig his vermin-eaten feet into the garbage. He bites his lower lip. Don't be surprised. It's not the child suffering, but Iningué tightening its bowels so as not to let the shit escape.

So it is for Yaya's son, the blind beggar. Well before the child was born, Yaya had seen that this would be the one who'd bring home the sorghum. He'd touched the full-moon belly of his wife, had laughed through his cola-teeth, then raised his arms to heaven: 'He'll bring the sorghum, he'll bring the sorghum – that is the Almighty's wish.' The child was born. First Yaya had put out one eye, but finding this act not enough to rouse pity, he put out the remaining eye. Then he prayed; his fingers entwined, he invoked heaven asking that leprosy devour the legs and arms of the child. Leprosy had not arrived. Yaya's hands had only contained a minuscule god.

Yaya's son grew up and was sent out into the street. Sometimes you meet him, groping his way along, tall, skinny in his dirty *boubou*, or sitting on the pavement, his legs crossed, his hands outstretched, softly chanting '*Allah kabia*', attracting the tourist's attention and inviting him to drop a few tears on the shoulders of Yaya's son. 'Such misery!' they'll say indignantly as they fulfil their works of charity. Then they'll forget. Everything is forgotten under the coconut trees. Even the blank stare of Yaya's son.

So it is for Ngono, the daughter of Ngala, who sent her to live with his brother in the city. He had given her a chicken. He told her that where his brother lived, there would be light, a school, a rich husband. He'll never know, Ngala, that down there his daughter, Ngono, continuously washes, swaddles and wipes the cousins. He'll never know that there his daughter's hands will be transformed into crocodile skin; that her dress, torn all the way up to the armpits is open to the penis of any guest who will tear her apart; that the chicken died before laying an egg. He'll never know that in Iningué only larvae grow from the earth.

So it is for the child – for all these children who are born adult and will never know how to measure the harshness of their destiny; these children who are widowers of their childhood, to whom even time no longer makes any promises.

And there, stretched out alone and restless, I tell myself that tomorrow I'll adopt one of them, for one must always begin with the first, the one who'll weed the path of love. I'll adopt Mala, nobody's son. I'll give him his forgotten childhood and everybody will remember, for the child-king must be remembered, he who must be carried on your back towards brightness, towards more light.

So there will be the house, the garden, the dog, the magpie at the end of the meadow, the children – one child already, Mala . . . And there will be Hassan, whom I shall see from my window, rushing towards me every evening, in the darkness of the setting sun.

My sister moans and turns over on her breast. A cloud gathers over my eyes. I fall asleep.

That night a nightmare attacks me. The children of Iningué are shorn. A ring is put through their noses. They're confined to the fields. They work under the whip of men with biceps as big as logs and skulls like bats. A legless woman takes care of the recalcitrant ones. Bound together hand and foot, they are entrusted to her. She beats them with her calloused hand, then sends them spinning into the sky three times, while chanting:

> 'Child, you do not exist.
> Child, you are born to obey.
> Child, you are born to be a slave to your parents.'

Then she throws them into the boa pit.

As for me, I work in silence and pray heaven to transform me. The miracle occurs. I become a gigantic plant with many heads. With my liana-tentacles, I collect the adults and smother them. I let go of my prey at their last spasm. I watch them – lips, eyes, nose, that heap of flesh washed by death. I find them beautiful. I bend over towards them, overcome by tenderness. I kiss them on the mouth, then return them to the dust. I weep. My tears wash the mud, give back the splendour of birth. All night long I walk around in my sealed off memory. A motionless bloody nuisance, I'm settling into destruction.

The following morning, as I open my eyes, I don't feel as if I've been dreaming. In Iningué, the dream is the imagination plugged into tomorrow. Doesn't anyone see the mothers tighten their belts in hunger? Tomorrow, they say, tomorrow there'll be bread, steaming coffee, water pouring from the sky. An enormous discrepancy. There's nothing but their feet crowding around in the mud making sucking sounds, and their husbands fucking off to the ministry where nothing ever gets done.

How is happiness made?

Me, I didn't dream. I notice the change as I wake up. An exacting sun. It's borrowing the windows of my body. It's penetrating my spirit. It's infiltrating everywhere. The time of machinations has come. The world is cracked. It needs to be glued together.

48

I jump out of bed. I throw on a dress, sandals. My eyes wander over the sleeping body of the girl, my sister. She's resting on one side, her cheek buried in the pillow, her hands clenched. Sometimes when I wake up and my sister's still asleep, I look at her body. It makes a backwards S. I love that S. A little bit more than anything else. Just a little bit. I can watch that S indefinitely. It's allowed. I can look, fill my eyes, get drunk on the S; look at it beyond the girl my sister, the white of the soles of her feet, her breasts, her thighs. Sometimes a miracle takes place. I lose my way. I no longer know where I am or who I am, but I know I'm not inside.

What is happiness like?

I look at my sister's body. The sleeping body of my sister. The deserted body of my sister. The talkative body of my sister. I'd have to use an infinite number of words to describe my sister's body. It is permitted to look – the eyes have no prescribed direction. Looking has always been the only satisfaction that I offer myself. At every birth, God ought to give a scalpel to the children – to dissect the rotting soul of their parents.

I slam the door of the room. I rush into the kitchen. Mother old one is there. She's putting two chicken drumsticks in a dish. She covers them with a newspaper. That's for the gentleman with the wound. She'll be seeing him this evening. Mother old one takes him the very best bits. As usual. The best bits are for the adults. 'That is to teach children to climb the walls of woe,' they state solemnly.

And tonight, mother old one will meet the man with the wound in the hut reserved for him by Mama Térecita.

And as usual, the man with the wound will be awaiting her, lying down, his penis in the air, his decayed ankle hanging down in the space between the bed and the wall. Some say that leprosy ate his ankle, others claim that it is because he stole eggs from his neighbour. He's chewing on a mouthful of snuff which he spits out profusely between two toothless bursts of laughter. Mother old one is still holding out the meat to him and says:

'Here.'

'Later,' he answers. 'The woman first.'

Mother old one lies down. Sometimes I follow her, I put my eye to the keyhole. I wait for the moment the bed creaks, when the cries

49

become louder. The bed laments, but no sound comes from the old woman's lips. He takes her very quickly, like an insect. He frees her, scratches his belly which hangs down to his thighs and says: 'I'm hungry, you've emptied me out.' Mother old one hurries up and gives him his meat. He eats and wipes his mouth on mother old one's *pagne*. He drinks his wine, he belches and tips her over again. She curls up in her pain.

Mother old one comes home well before dawn. She wants to remain the widow of her husband, the one who with her nerves on edge with impatience, waits for the day she'll join him among the dead. She scrapes along against a wall. When a neighbour surprises her between two compounds, she says: 'I was just peeing'. He smiles.

When mother old one is angry because the gentleman with the wound went wandering off into another hole, she hollers. She kicks him on the wound. He screams. People come running – they cheer her on. She smacks him with the flat of her hand, sometimes with a pestle. The next morning she comes back with the food he hasn't eaten. She says to us:

'A mother must always provide food for her children. I've saved yesterday's left-overs for you.'

We open the package. We discover it's the same meat that's come back. It's gone bad.

That particular morning, when mother old one senses me in her space, she stops bustling about and the corners of her mouth tighten. She tries to hide the drumsticks. She pours herself a bowl of coffee and sits down at the small table. I sit down across from her. My eyes take in the window letting the day filter in. She drinks her coffee, mother old one, her fists clenched around her bowl. She tries to catch my eye. I elude her though I won't look down. And I, the excluded girlchild-woman, I know that my eyes will not be lowered again. They will unite with the green fruit on the tree while waiting for it to ripen. However, it seems to me that the name of Monsieur John rises from mother old one's lips. The sound of his cash hits me with every gulp. He divides himself up. He is joined again around me; he closes in on me, horizontally, vertically. He traps me. I struggle. I baulk at the idea that money alone, clean or dirty, allows us to live. Cash – love. Cash – love. I must choose. I despise those who have both; I hate those who have everything. I puke on their happiness and the air about them that says: 'Come share in my joy since I'm happy.'

Sometimes I'd like to put them to sleep forever, with their happiness and their money; put an end to their rapture once and for all. But they always wake up. So then I console myself by thinking that it is they who have been swindled by God the Creator. He's allotted them the time needed to live life and the time needed to die, but not what is needed to die and be born at the same time. Me – I died at my birth.

I waver for many long minutes. Divine, Human. Good, Evil. Shadow, light. Between them I see a papier mâché frontier. I hesitate – there's no recipe with which to concoct certainties any more. For self-reconciliation resembles a quest for friendship. Friends do not unite. They agree to spend a rainy afternoon between empty or bountiful truths. Together they trudge along roads in bloom or through the desert. They search for the mystery that must be safeguarded or the material to be remodelled. Sometimes you'll surprise them in their laughter or their tears. They've just invented eternity or hatred.

'Have you thought about yesterday?' mother old one says, interrupting my train of thought.

'Yes.'

'So what are you going to do?'

'Nothing; I'm waiting.'

'For what?'

I don't want to talk to her about my decision to adopt Mala, to give him his stolen childhood. I don't want to talk to her about Hassan, the house, the magpie at the end of the meadow. I resort to vagueness and say in a soft voice:

'I'm waiting for something. I don't know its name, but it will whisper to me, inside.'

'Ungrateful girl.'

'Let me live.'

'You'll croak with your mouth wide open, you will.'

Right on target! Her last arrow brings me down. She's just flung open the chaotic repertoire of the future for me. She's just unearthed

51

my tragedy. I don't want to hear her; I must not hear her. The image of mother old one shaking her mat out over the ruins of my life must be chased away. The backwater needs time to hollow out its bed. The pool of water needs time to begin to flow.

I lower my head. Silence. A long while goes by – a long time during which the conflicting sounds of our thoughts and the knot of sadness fill the space, make happiness grow old. I rise. I shake out my dress as if to get rid of my fleas.

I say: 'Ma, I'm going out.' Mother old one looks at me, her eyes narrow with anger.

'You're going to give it away again for free, that backside of yours *djô*?'

I don't respond. A mission awaits me. To find Mala again.

◆

Mala. He was born twelve years earlier from a merry little sperma-tozoon. His mother, who had a shop in the upper district, let various men take their turn and ride her as the waves ride the sea. He was born. She said that a child for a woman of her kind was the 'gift of evil' and that she needed to 'let the devil finish his work'. She put him in a cardboard box, gave him terror to suckle, locked him up in her little room and disappeared. For several days Mala rolled around in his faeces. Neighbours finally came in. Maggots had achieved the act of darkness: they had devoured a part of his legs. He was entrusted to his grandmother, a senile old woman who concocted and sold corn alcohol. She nicknamed him 'Foot-wreck'.

Foot-wreck . . . His life fitted completely into the misery that dwelt in him. The evil eye lived in him. Some insist they've seen him transform himself into a snake. Others into an adult. Whenever he heard this, he'd raise his pus-filled eyes and roll them backwards, grimacing hideously. The slanderer would run off yelling: 'He's cursed, he's cursed! he tried to murder me!' Foot-wreck would burst out laughing.

Foot-wreck. He justified his life with the terror he inspired. He'd wash once a year to please Santa Claus and hang a sandal on a branch to catch his eye. Every time he felt the night approach, spreading its seed in children's memories, he'd make the gesture in which the hope of ecstasy lay inscribed. In vain. Santa Claus would pass by, forgetting him.

The rest of the time he'd dirty himself with soot and draw on a moustache to make himself look grown-up. He said that this way he was addressing the wait formally and no longer searching for Santa Claus' footsteps in the sand or in the clouds. He'd spend his days hobbling through the streets, preparing survival plans, chasing skirts, and emptying the dregs from wine and beer bottles in cafés. One day he met Monsieur Difé, a war hero who had left his lower abdomen on the battlefield. Monsieur Difé rumpled his hair with the one arm he had left, lowered his pants to show his paralysis, wept over the absence of his scrotum, over his wish to have a son, over the joy a child brings. Foot-wreck listened to him and came to the conclusion that he'd do well to let himself flop down somewhere to bring some laughter into his life. He went from house to house asking for a father, a mother. He was welcomed with overripe tomatoes and buckets of water. He kidnapped a baby and took refuge with him underneath a bridge. His hands were gentle, his movements caressing. All day long he played daddy. Iningué was mobilised. Round-ups and searchparties were organised to find the baby. Foot-wreck brought him back just before nightfall. He was tied hand and foot and whipped. When they set him free, he guffawed, an idiotic laughter, and said: 'I've been dreaming!'

I walk down the street letting my thoughts drift towards Mala. At this hour of the day the streets are teeming with life. Schoolkids, looking cramped in their green, red or yellow uniforms, satchels under their arms, are singing as they go: 'Are you sleeping, are you sleeping, Brother Banana? Morning bells are ringing'. Matrons, with babies on their backs, and balancing basins on their heads, are hurrying towards the market-place as they squawk. Old men, haphazardly spread out on mats under the verandas, chew tobacco while they await the eternal abyss. To whomever is willing to listen they ramble on: 'The soil of this city is rotten. In my village it is red and springy. It knows how to feed my bones.' Sometimes I listen to them, laughter rising at the back of my throat. They seem to forget, these tired old men, they seem to forget they were the first whores of Iningué. Before, when their blood was young and their penises would rise at dawn, they'd run after riches, in the hope of accumulating more and more. Today they arrive out of breath from having been fucked over by the city, their eyes heavy-lidded and their hands empty, soliciting the impossible in order to deceive death: the right – what they call their right – to rest one day underneath the earth they have abandoned.

◆

An old shack of sheet metal and brick. Dirty. Courtyard strewn with rubbish. Mala's house. I go in without knocking. A smell of mildew and excrement hits me in the face. I move forward into the room; I put a hand up above my eyes in order to get accustomed to the semi-darkness. Some figures are slumped in dilapidated armchairs scattered here and there; with gullets turned up, a grey look on their faces and their hands trembling, they're getting smashed on small glasses of corn whiskey which they empty in one gulp. Some of them are snoring as they chew the side of their mouths, wrapped around their own excrement. In the centre of the room the bench that serves as a table is loaded with empty bottles and especially with glasses that are chipped from selling alcohol. Sitting in a corner is Djana the madman, his eyes popping out of his head. He is pummelling old newspapers with feverish hands, as he recites his rosary: 'Y djani silaba, y djani silaba. Y titinini y titinini fifty. Y titinini y titinini sixty.' I stand still in front of him. The smell on him of alcohol and rancid ham goes right through me. I let old habits come to my rescue. I subject my neck to my will. I force it to bend. I read: 'Hostilities in the Middle East. Soviet invasion of Afghanistan. The forgotten people of Bangladesh.' I no longer budge. I garner the rebellion these words sow in me. I'm watching for things to snap. The apocalypse. Nothing. Not even any despair. There's trouble brewing. Today, only onions make people weep.

'Careful,' one of the raised gullets, whose lips scorched from the alcohol look like a chicken's asshole, says to me. 'You, too, will end up crazy.'

I turn to him with questioning eyes. He bursts out laughing,

54

scratches at his testicles, and explains to me that Djana was made crazy by books.

I let a few moments flow by, twist my lips, and then answer: 'Foolishness ends up by making reason and madness equals.'

He opens his mouth but I am no longer there to hear him. I go over to Foot-wreck's grandmother, who is sitting on the kitchen table, busily emptying the dregs from every glass. As soon as she sees me, she stands up on her scrawny paws, their nails encrusted with filth, and extends one hand full of fissures and boils as she scratches her armpit with the other. She rolls her yellow eyes and gives me her biggest stump-toothed smile.

'I'm so pleased to see you, my girl, what a surprise! You'll be coming more often, I hope. There's nothing like young flesh to attract customers.'

I turn my eyes away. Revulsion winds around my tongue. My head is spinning. I breathe deeply to silence anger – the appropriate thing to do as a new wisdom dawns. I smile. I tell her I'll come as often as I'm able but that today I'd like to speak to Mala.

'What do you want with that son of a whore?'

'I'd like to speak to him, Ma!'

'You've got some money for him?'

'No, Ma. But . . .'

'He's over there,' she says, sucking noisily on one of her stumpy teeth. With her hand she motions to a figure huddled up on a mat. 'He's a big mouth to feed for a poor old woman like me. It's been two moons since his mother gave us any money at all.'

Mala is sleeping – curled up with his fists tightly over his eyes. I approach him on tiptoe so as not to awaken him too abruptly. I stop and observe him for a long while – filling my eyes with his restfulness in order to steal the most precious image of him. I crouch down and tap him on the cheek. He opens his eyes and closes them just as quickly. I begin anew, he grumbles, I make the gesture of love, he leaps up on his behind.

'Shit! What do you want from me, eh?'

I'm nonplussed. It all comes to a halt – the harmony of the words I'd been repeating to myself to reinvent the music of eternity. I rise, pretend to go away.

'Not so fast, Gâ,' he says, shaking himself. 'You didn't wake Foot-wreck for nothing now, did you?'

'. . .'

'If you want me to carry bags, Foot-wreck has more armed forces in his arms than any band of cops. Look at Foot-wreck's fingers – they're cracked in the middle. Foot-wreck is strong. And if it's a secret you're concerned about, Foot-wreck is mute.'

'Nothing like that. I want to take care of you.'

These words paralyse space. The shadow stops its dance and crystallises all around us. I smile. I take his hand, grimy and sticky from the street. I kiss each finger, and tense with emotion I say:

'From now on, you won't be walking alone any more. I'll be there. I shall bring you the dream; I'll raise you in the gentleness of the world.'

He looks at me.

'You're crazy, Gâ,' he says, 'completely insane! The devil must live inside you, too.'

He scrutinises me with half-closed eyes, shrugs his shoulders, barks something like 'really now', takes a cigarette stub out from his raggedy clothes, lights it and bursts out laughing. Words spout forth from his mouth, solidifying around me to snuff out my joy. I don't understand. I grab him by his hair, tell him that he must express some basic respect owed any mother; that he must take a bath. He resists, I pull harder, snivelling he says 'Yes, Ma'. I let go of him. He grabs my hand as if to kiss it. I feel his teeth digging deeply into my flesh. I barely have time to let out a cry when his crippled footsteps are already moving away.

I smother my rage. I yell: 'Wretched child!' The lifted gullets ululate. I see their murky images, heavy with dirt, envelop the room in a cloak of black moonlight. They say that Foot-wreck is inhabited by more demons than all of Africa's starving children put together. They say that in any event there are more worms in his belly than in that of any street dog and that he'll soon be going back to where he came from: the darkness. The grandmother crosses herself, kneels down and recites several *Ave Marias*, fiddling with her amulet before she bursts into sobs. She weeps, spluttering that God is everywhere but that his footsteps came to a halt when he reached her doorstep.

She says he put her here by mistake, but that the time has come to implore the heavens to cut her throat and put an end to her misery. Everyone gets up, fractious but stimulated by alcoholic solidarity. Some suggest she have a drink. 'It helps,' they say; others belch and join in the chorus cursing the child.

I let these moments pass. I don't move. I say nothing. I let my body find new composure. I'm thinking that from now on I'd better take care of it, for the road to heaven will be a very long one. I go out into the street, into the sunlight.

◆

The day is already well on its way. I move on in its brightness, trying to chase away the visions of Foot-wreck. Little girls are crowding the cracked pavements, offering their charms and their bowls of peanuts to passers-by. Some of these seem shocked and tell them to wait a few more years to give the bark of the hevea time to become lubricated; the girls answer with crystalline laughter, showing their behinds in exaggerated movements, and protest, saying that waiting in Iningué is a form of suicide. As for the youngest ones among them, barely three seasons old, they're nibbling on green mangoes as they wait for the runs to begin which will return them to dust. And they croak, these kids. So many of them succumb that the women make more and more of them. Multiply themselves. Leave their mark. Beat them up. Get around destiny. In Iningué, the woman has forgotten the child, the gesture that brings love – she's just an egg-laying hen. She says: 'A child is the security of old age'. Besides, the governor himself hands out medals to women who have large families. For service rendered to the fatherland. Mother old one tried to be crowned. If I focus my eyes on the past, I see her still, wide-assed in her *kaba*, coming and going, preparing celebration meals between light laughter and alacrity. Mother old one, as sprightly as in the springtime of her fifteenth season. She has strangled ten chickens, fifteen ducks. The drum is beating outside, and the cousins of cousins from the village are jigging about and refreshing themselves with palm wine. Some of them are rolling in the dust, on the pretext they are the spirits of the ancestors who've come to share the festivities. Others – quiet drunkards – are silently nursing their Hâ. The women clap their hands, loudly vocalising their *Ywééé*s. Sometimes one of them takes advantage of the general bloody rot to occupy some forbidden nesting space. The others turn into ostriches. Nothing seen. Nothing heard.

Mother old one has treated her hair with lime. It's glued to her head like the feathers on a wet chicken. All night long she's fussing about, scouring and cleaning, while the cousins, oozing gluttony, stuff their bellies. And well before daylight, we take the road of the coronation.

The laying hens are there. As proud as geese in a market-place. Muzzled women. Happy to be heroines, thanks to acts of everyday life. I see them again. The look in their eyes ecstatic. Mouths wide. Vague gestures. Their chatter shatters around me and envelops me in images, awakening in me the desire to cut off my breasts to gather up my buttocks and cut the Gordian knots.

At three in the afternoon, the governor arrives. Greasy. Dripping. He lisps. High level. Colourless speech. It's hard to live without any colour. The laying hens remember 'For the service rendered to the fatherland'.

The governor forgets to cite mother old one.

But it can only be an oversight, according to her. A simple omission. At first, every day at the same time she'd sit right down on the floor. She's listening to the radio. She listens to every station, in every possible and imaginable language. Are they speaking about someone with the same first name or the same last name? She lets out a few *Ywééé*s. She claps her hands. The veranda fills up with the curious.

'What's her problem?'

'I'm going to be crowned! I'm getting a medal! Oh, my God, what happiness!'

'She's crazy,' the crowd comments. 'That's because she ate that herb to make her man love her.' 'Poor woman. She doesn't deserve this.' 'Eh, now, everyone always gets what he deserves. Feet where they belong, in the mud, head where it belongs, in the sky. That's the way it all goes in life.'

They begin to disperse, puffed-up with contempt and pity.

Left alone, mother old one looks around, broken by her failure to comprehend. I come close to her, take her hand and take her to her room, on to her bed. Mother old one protests – she wants to be left alone with her upside down dreams. I leave on tiptoe, pursued by her sobs.

For the old woman, being crowned is an idea upon which she has hung her very breath. Same effect as the herb. Always by her side. Some nights when the moon is full, she gets up, tattoos her face with lipstick and goes out into the courtyard naked. She rolls around on the ground and eats dust to ward off the curse put on her by those who are jealous. She confirms that the whole of Iningué is jealous of her belly that has carried twelve children. Ten of them died? What difference does that make – she still had twelve children. I don't tell her that death, which is incorruptible, has extinguished all warmth in her and that her ten children lie forever underneath a sterile earth. No jealousy to be feared. I keep quiet. I have to keep quiet. Sometimes, with grief in my guts, I hide behind a pile of rubbish. I don't whimper. Tears no longer serve any purpose. I put my head in my hands. I breathe deeply. I wait for the adult who'll come to me, put his hands on my shoulders and stroke my hair. Nobody comes. I close my eyes even more tightly, towards the dream, the elsewhere. Only then do I rise into the sky, between white sheets, to the heart of birds.

One morning, she decides to send a letter to the governor to remind him of his omission.

My very dear, well-beloved Governor, good day.

It is a forgotten mother who writes to you. How is your health and that of your children?

No great problems here. As for me, I am not in good health. You forgot to call me the other day to give me a medal and this is bothering me a lot; now I can no longer sleep. So, my son, I am coming to you now, to solicit your high-placed goodwill and arrange for this to happen quickly. And if you do not come, who would you wish to send in your place? You are the leader of us all. Other than that, all is well. I have made twelve kids and God took ten of them back. And I'll give my belly up to life if God wants it so. And God will want it so since my insides are clean and very beautiful. I have never done any harm to anyone. Other than that, all is well. I continue to do a little business to feed the two children I have left. My husband pays no attention to anything. You know how it is these days – he secretly goes to visit another woman and looks at me as if I'm scum. The person who will give you this letter will also give you some money for transportation, which I have given him for you. And if you cannot come, give him the medal to bring to me. My very dear Governor president, I am leaving you now, wishing you and your children good health. Don't forget to say hello to your wife on my behalf. My children greet you.

Signed by us, Ngâ Taba.
A forgotten mother.

She writes every week. The same words. The same length. She puts no stamp and no address on the envelope. She throws her letters on the runway of the airport so that the planes will pick them up. When her attention is drawn to this, she looks at the ground, nothing but the ground, and says: 'It says *by air* on the envelope'.

At that time I didn't know that the survival instinct is much like this plaintive exaggeration, like this sorrow designed as a stage production might be, in order for woman to resign herself to death while denying it all along the way.

In the cell, the flame of the candle flickers. Anna-Claude shudders. She feels dizzy. Never has she felt so wedded to the secret movements of the other. Every word, every gesture of the dying woman is like so much fluid liberating her life, introducing her into a world where her person is being given a meaning, is creating for her a new destiny – of other pasts; a heritage of successive lives. With her deepening knowledge of Tanga, she brings back uninhabited periods of time, forgotten practices, formed under the reign of hatred. She tells herself that she stands at the frontier of eternity and that it is her role to bequeath to men the fermentations of History, in order to paint the frescoes of love in homage to the unknown woman. Perhaps heaven will create a diversion as she stands on the edge of the precipice and send her Ousmane.

She came to Africa to bring him out of hiding. For months, she criss-crossed the land, burrowed into it, hollowed it out, and out of the exhausting desire to clasp hold of what was slipping away, she asked heaven for the herb of oblivion to be put on the wounds of her dream. Nothing appeared. Instead, the hyenas of Iningué's misery gathered around her – its fallen spectres, its tattered horizons, its vibrations of suffering. She cursed it, this wretchedness. In the name of equality. In the name of the range of laws to be dispensed. In the name of the human being who must follow man as his shadow. But now here is this wretchedness filling her soul, which until now she has lived out through her body. She's under the impression that she inhabits it with all her despair as cohort, which is similar to a dawnless day. A day. A light, nevertheless, which allows her to place herself, to know herself while the demented pursuit of Ousmane – that incessant continuation of the dream – didn't bring her any self-definition, since she was too busy mounting the ladder of unrest.

Tanga opens her mouth.

'I see what you're thinking.'

'And what do you see?'

'You're learning to make an abstraction of your body, to feel with your soul.'

'And how do you know that? Don't tell me you have a third eye.'

'Do you know what mango trees do at night when they're sure the people are asleep?'

'No.'

'They become men; they act like them, and at the second crowing of the cock, they pick up their bark again, kiss each other, wink at each other, and go to sleep in order to hand life back over to humans.'

'A lovely fable!'

Tanga makes a distraught movement with her hand.

'That's what you have to do in order to get to know this earth and its inhabitants better.'

'Die with you, for example.'

'For example.'

'I don't want to die.'

'I'm not asking you to die. I want you to become a bird, to soar over the world, torment the wind, and make dreams fly over every pillow – that's all. But for now, I want to tell you about my death.'

'I don't want to know about that. What interests me is your story.'

'And yet my death is much like yours. It is the same for everybody, you know? She has a prudish body which uncovers itself and tears itself apart – innocent flesh which becomes denuded, eviscerated, under skilful hands. She's the nose that wants to be stopped up when faced with excrement. Sometimes, she is mute and then,' the dying woman adds as she clicks her tongue, 'she is interesting. She doesn't see the body; she doesn't see the sheets; she becomes the evening inviting us into her arms to soothe our soul . . .'

'Be quiet!'

'Why be quiet, woman? I must die, so at least allow this dead woman to open her eyes and contemplate the crowd of those who weep over me. I look to my right, to my left. How about that – it's a desert! Eh, no! Nobody will miss me; nobody will clean my tomb of its weeds.'

'Your mother is there.'

'Don't make me laugh. I filled her belly. My role is finished. Today I no longer exist for her.'

'I'll be there.'

'You're not from this land. You won't know how.'

'You despise me.'

'No. But there are certain things that are passed on from one generation to the next. They're not acquired.'

'I know that I know. Intuition.'

'Stop your nonsense.'

'No! You seem to forget that blood is neither white nor black. It's quite simply red.'

Tanga doesn't answer. A long while goes by – empty, hollow. Suddenly she says to Anna-Claude that it is time to pick up the story where she left off. And once again, words filled the space.

◆

Leaving Foot-wreck that day, I let my thoughts drift to mother old one and her silliness, then I forget her. The sun is beating down and there is a strong smell in the street. Everywhere there are smells of smoked fish, beer, peanuts and dead rats, all mixed together, churned up in nausea. I'm strolling along, meditating over these emanations of grub and filth. I tell myself they're like man, united with him in the process of decomposition. This idea wrings my insides. I'm disgusted with myself. I walk on, hating every one of my woman's footsteps. Steps of a woman or of carrion? I'm like that – I feed on what stinks and produces maggots. A rotten stray. A lost dog. I am a grain of sand, the bark of a leafless tree.

Yet I love to walk. I have always thought that feet are the wings of the universe – the thought that they carry the individual towards regions of bloom has always been inside me. As a child, I would sometimes walk slowly, heavily, enjoying my steps like pieces of chocolate I'd let melt on my tongue so the pleasure would last longer. But these feet coming back from Foot-wreck's place seem to be weighed down with mud. They're wolfing down my dreams and bringing me useless thoughts. They're carrying me down blind roadways, towards nothingness. I'm not saying this to justify what's coming, besides I'm not making any excuses for that. But I like the air that smells of knowledge. Making no sense? I don't give a damn. Sometimes, I'd like to be Christ, daughter of blocked out light, of the shadow that brightens. I'd like it so much if the pace of unhappiness would stop! I'd like the outlines of a new life to be sketched for me in which I'd offer to be a mother to the child who needs one – to other children as well – a man, the house, the dog, the magpie at the end of the meadow. Is that too much to ask? Christ didn't have any balls either.

◆

I continue walking in the streets. I let grief and weariness move me along – lead me to unidentified places. I'm thinking; I don't know what my destiny is, but I do know that I want to understand, to live, to rediscover my earlier state of mind when, suddenly, the idea occurs to me that there's nothing on this earth that doesn't have its counterpart in heaven. I tell myself that if all this is only so I can live a dog's life in heaven, I'd rather turn my sights on the devil. I turn around. I go to the market-place. It is crowded – women selling spices, vegetables, beignets, old books.

Cars drive by, almost running over housewives who jump aside twittering. Police on patrol, truncheon in hand, disperse illicit vendors. I continue on my way between rows of tomatoes and yams, my body damp, my nerves on edge. From time to time, my sandals get stuck in the *poto-poto*. I pull them out, spattering women who're flopped down in front of pyramids of vegetables. They grumble, accompanying my steps with cries of 'Careful, you dirty whore.' I turn around. I tell them I'm no longer careful because my father raped me. They're not surprised.

The other end of the market-place. A large building chewed up by time: the slaughterhouse. I come close enough to stick my nose against its window, brown with filth. Greyish walls. Big green flies. Carcasses hanging from hooks. A man, stiff in a white apron smudged with stains, is struggling to carve up a pig. He stops at regular intervals, breathes heavily and wipes his forehead with a sweeping movement of his hairy hand before he starts his carnage again. I watch him. With vague images that come to me. Childhood's slashed throat. Life disembowelled.

A memory.

Mother old one is in the village. I sleep with father old one. I wake up. The middle of the night. Filtered light. Mosquitoes. Father old one's body at rest. I slip my hand underneath the mattress. A box with matches. I open it. Ticks inside. I catch one with a single motion. I put it on father old one's neck. It bites, sucks, swells up. When it's sated, it falls down on the sheet. I crush it. Blood on my fingers. Blood in my hands. Broken destinies. Dying body dreaming of drinking life, growing in order to become beautiful, to be adult so as not to suffer any more.

I cross my legs, cross my hands, close my eyes. I'm waiting for those substances to penetrate me that strengthen and make me grow. Hope, wait for me. I'm running to you. Open your gate. In the back of your flowerless garden one leaf is sleeping.

Father old one wakes up.

'What're you doing, eh? You're not sleeping?'

'No, Pa. I'm not sleepy.'

He leaps up, sits on his behind, furious and foists his flaccid flesh upon me.

'You look at me while I'm sleeping, you sorceress, you dirty little witch,' he screams. 'Get out! Get the hell out right now!'

Why this sudden loss of control? Why this vulnerability in front of me? In this world that trots around on its hands, anxiety creates gaps in everyone's behaviour.

Stung to the core, I leave his room. I stop in the living room. I look at the ceiling, nothing but the ceiling. I question it about the secret of its height: all the rains of Iningué may shed their water over me – I'm not growing. Farewell, hope. I have got the time wrong, maybe the wrong place. My breath has chased away the leaf in your garden. Farewell, my friend. No hard feelings.

◆

That day, after leaving Foot-wreck, I spend a long time watching the hairy butcher. Violence. Despair. My fiancés. They possess me. I push open the door of the slaughterhouse. I go in. Smell of dead cattle, blood, mildew. I allow my eyes time to get used to the semi-darkness. I scrutinise the man. Frizzy hair. Arched eyebrows ... Thick lips. I go over to him. He doesn't raise his head. My heart tightens. I cough and ask him in a small voice:

'Could you do me a favour?'

'What's that?' he asks without stopping gutting the pig.

'Lock me up with the cattle or cut my throat, please.'

'And why should I do that?'

'I want to get to know them, yes to know them so I don't have to love people any more.'

Without leaving him time to digest this, to understand, I get undressed, lie down on the table and offer him my neck. He raises his knife. I close my eyes, I wait. Flies settle down on me and taunt me. I notice the wriggling of their feet on my eyelids, my nose, my mouth. I've just rediscovered my natural state: BEAST OF BURDEN.

Time stands still; it's hot. It clings, delivers the present moment. A dog howls. I open my eyes. There's the butcher, his weary fists on his hips.

'You're one of those girls I detest,' he says dully. 'Woman or child? You're one of those who generates nothing but shit. Get the hell out.'

My courage gone, I quickly throw on my clothes and attempt a backwards retreat with my hands stretched out.

'Hey there! Not so fast,' he thunders.

With two steps he's there and he grabs me around the waist.

'Let go of me! Let me go!'

'Oh no! When your parents let you loiter around the streets, surely they mean you to be of service, eh?'

'Please, please.'

'Shut up! My loins have been needing release for weeks now. You'll serve just fine to start me off.'

He lowers the straps of my dress. He kneels down. Greedily he sucks my breasts. I settle into my role as improvised mamma. He assaults me. Sweet mamma, so sweet. And the house, the dog, the magpie at the end of the meadow. And the butcher-child. But what is that suddenly flooding my breasts? Is it the sea drawing waves draped across my back? No, not so. It is the butcher-man crying. What can I do, what can I do, other than to add one word to another just to put a bit of colour into life's blackness.

'Come now, don't cry, calm down.'

'I can't, I can't help it.'

'A man, a real man, never lets a tear drop.'

'You can't become a man without having first been a child, you understand?'

Yes, I understand. I'd like for him to be so happy that he'd die from it! but I no longer feel like listening to others and their problems. Too much sorrow dwells in me. There's no room for his! I readjust my clothes. I go out into the sun, fleeing this madman's place, saved from my own madness.

◆

The sun is at its zenith. I'm hot. I don't want to go home. A question turns around and around inside me – always the same one: 'Why didn't Mala want anything to do with me?' No answer. The city is blazing around me, a stranger. I walk around aimlessly, celebrating my contest with desolation without anyone to witness it. What good does it do to run around offering happiness since nobody wants any part of it? Someone put on earth by God to be married to uselessness can kick the bucket no matter where.

As I turn the corner into an alley, a man collides with me. He smiles, his look inviting. Without needing to exchange a word, I understand that at that very moment the tension of our bodies is the same. I get up and submit to his desire underneath a porch. I'd like for our pleasures to meet. I unfurl my flesh. No feeling. Colourless. The classic blow. I focus my senses on the house, the garden, the magpie at the end of the meadow, children, Hassan. I, girlchild-woman, I know that my memory shouldn't lose sight of them, for when once satiated, the man abandons me on the brink of my anxieties, my body will have to go on searching for the impossible: the house, the garden, the dog, children, the magpie at the end of the meadow, Hassan.

Sweat against sweat, I go along with the stranger to the point of vertigo, between the coming and going of dreams that run into each other. He sets me free; he loses me. I find myself vanquished again, forgotten as always.

'Shall we see each other again?'

'No.'

'Are you married?'

'Yes.'

'My wife is very young as well. Thirteen. She's expecting a baby. It worries me a lot, I keep wondering where it's going to come out.'

'You should've thought about that earlier.'

He shrugs his shoulders and readjusts his trousers. What is there to say in a country where everything, even the air, is a prison? I go back out into the sun.

The street is deserted. Only a few street kids roam around, dragging their feet. They come out with laughter as tired as their feet as they make comments about my behind. In the streets, empty in the early afternoon, there's nothing but the buzzing of fat green flies above the garbage cans. I walk slowly, ponderously. I want to grasp the morning's events, drown them in lush vegetation, to live at last. My future can't afford to take any more time. But in Iningué, all that the earth produces is pain like a growth in the flesh.

◆

I arrive at our house. Mother old one is flopped down on a mat. She's shelling pistachios. Next to her, the girl my sister. Around her she has constructed a woman's framework. Kohl around the eyes. Painted mouth. Skin smeared with talcum powder. Wig. I look at her. The red miniskirt, black patent leather shoes on three-inch high heels, mother old one's old red plastic purse which she lugs about and swings in the air. She looks important and solemn in the way she moves, the girl my sister. The tips of her adolescent breasts jiggle. The rest is motionless. No flesh. Every ten steps, her feet twist almost to the point of dislocation. I stay there staring, speechless, eyes riveted on the whys, the what's going on heres, with that look only the down and out understand.

Five minutes? Ten minutes? I'm eclipsed. Mother old one is too.

There is no longer anything but the girl my sister, made smaller by a short flashy dress, who's heading towards the settings that I know – the men, those washouts with nothing to offer until the breaking point is reached.

'What do you think of me, Big One? Aren't I pretty?' she asks me as she struts around.

'D'you really want to know?'

'Yes.'

I look her over from top to toe, then direct my gaze at the street, searching for the words with which to pulverise ugliness, kill madness. Waste purity or waste breath, what's the difference? I've been a child-whore from the beginning. But for my sister I wanted a life made to the measure of the dreams my head has been filled with. Sometimes I'd imagine her in a tennis outfit, racket in hand, moving her body around in the gardens of a palace. Was that too much to ask? In our life, we needed a window, offering something, something to dream about. Just so you could get the impression you were living life to the full.

'You're not answering me, Big One. Why not?'

'You really want me to?'

'Well . . . Yes. It's important.'

'You shouldn't be worrying about that at your age.'

'What should it be at my age?'

'Go and learn to read. That's what'll save you.'

'What do you take me for? An idiot?'

'No. But your body still smells of milk.'

I've hardly pronounced those words when her complexion turns grey. Her face takes on that murderous look and she screams and shouts:

'You're just jealous! Jealous! Dirty slut. Why don't you drop dead?'

I don't understand her. Her words resound inside my skull like a peal of bells. She bends over to me. Our breath meets. I back away.

'You're scared, aren't you? You're afraid that I'll steal your Monsieur John. Tell her, Ma, go ahead and tell her that Monsieur John is about to take me out for a drive.'

I'm perplexed. Bolts pop off in my head. I'm losing myself! An explosion of identity. Searching for oneself in death to get to know birth! Beginning with the origins in order to understand the end! Inventing a detail, patching it up and adjusting it to suit one's destiny. No, and no again! I am young and my genitals are wrinkled. I turn my head towards mother old one. Perhaps . . . She looks down to her withered hands. She picks up a fistful of pistachios. She puts one in her mouth. She cracks it. She spits it out again. She starts anew, again and again . . .

Me, girlchild-woman, I would have liked it as a reading, to have had it dictated out loud, repeated in a thousand ways just to reassure myself that my mind hadn't gone. But my sister's words are there, sparkling with madness, engraved in my flesh in letters of fire. Suddenly I feel heavy – heavy from having loved her, heavy with this adolescent body, heavy with inadmissible regrets. It seems to me that the light is suddenly mimicking the shade, suggesting that my sister's figure is undesirable. Hurt, with my body out of joint, I go towards my room, my heart and eyes closed. I want to distance myself from my sister's childhood, that bewildered childhood, stretched out towards the dusk. I want to flee, to sever every link, our memories, our mutual belonging. To sleep with rage. To sleep beyond delirium. To sleep. I enter my room. Just as I'm about to close the door, mother old one yells in my direction:

'You'd better learn to share the goods, my girl!'

Despair locks her words away.

Once I'm alone, I curl up – a good posture in which to look beyond oneself, to direct your thoughts somewhere else. The house. Children. The dog. The magpie at the end of the meadow. The man. Kisses. Tobacco. Scents. Everything becomes a sterile list. All that's left is fear and disgust with the departing dream.

Little by little I enter a strange drowsiness. I'm sleeping or awake. I am elsewhere. I'm walking around a country where trees talk, visit one another, and as dusk begins to fall they welcome their beloved to renew their gestures of love. The streets are full of waterlilies which, with one gesture, place their hands on my tilted cheek and tell me the secrets of my mother the stars. I do not understand; I say to myself that perhaps there is no spirit, only wretchedness and the void. So, I turned my head towards memories.

Before, when I was to meet a rich man, I'd warn mother old one. We'd get organised for my departure. The house would be mobilised. Cantankerous, mother old one would stand at my right and direct the operation. 'Your sister's shoes!' she'd thunder for the benefit of my sibling, or 'Her comb!' or 'Her shawl!' The girl my sister would scurry around, scramble underneath her bed, behind the closet, and fish out a pair of sandals, a pencil, lipstick. As for me, I'd paint my eyes and my lips. I'd grab a mirror. I'd call forth the idea of the image I wanted of myself. It would present itself, fuzzy with uncertainties. Mother old one would lose her patience, prance around.

'Hurry up, or else you're going to miss him.'

'Calm down, Ma. Even if I'm late, he'll wait.'

'You'd better take advantage of this, my girl, because once time starts eating away at you, ha ha . . . Nobody'll be waiting for you any more. Not even a dog.'

I'd listen to her, seeing myself in ruins, a scarecrow that would keep even the vultures away. Sometimes I'd stretch my lips out, grimace to see how the claws of time might do their job. Mother old one would watch me at length, her eyes plugged into yesterday. Me, girlchild-woman, I knew the woman wanted to have the time back again when her breasts were pointed and her legs supple. Her gaze would become blurred with tears. I'd take her by the arm. I'd lead her to the nearest easy chair. She'd let herself fall and would burst out sobbing.

'What's going to become of me, my girl, what's going to become of me?'

'As long as I can move my ass, there's no problem.'

'You won't leave me to fend for myself, eh, my girl?'

'No, Ma.'

'Swear it.'

'I swear.'

She'd throw herself on my hands which she'd cover with blessings as she'd chant, 'Long life to you, my daughter; long life to men,' and 'Thank you, Lord.'

She still had her heaven waiting at the end.

Me, I had to continue my task. To work out how to use my charms.

Money, money for the old woman. Be pleasing. Be pleasing. Be pleasing. The idea became an obsession. Yet, I knew full well that covering the body mattered little since it would be undressed in order to forget the shadow. I'd dress it with care. It was clean. It was desirable. I lived for it alone. I hated it. Depressed, I'd drag it around the streets, my attention fixed on these bands of men, adolescent, young, old – these men who were incapable of moving up from ass to heart. Powerless when it came to feelings. Nothing but their penis raised like a magic wand. I'd pass by; I'd count them. One. Two. Three thousand. The tumour of cities. Filthy. Greasy. They'd emerge within my field of vision, grazing, wrinkled, beardless. They'd take over from each other around me, on top of me . . . An assembly line. Eyes like billiard balls. Vice screwed into my loins. Love? Never! Sometimes, when I felt courageous enough to talk, I'd plunk myself in front of one of them and let fly: 'And what about a little tenderness, asshole!' He'd draw back, horrified, put his index finger to his temple: 'But . . . but she's completely nuts!'

I wouldn't answer. I'd let my body distance itself from my head. I'd take off my shoes. I'd walk on the asphalt. My feet would burn. I wouldn't cry. That was reserved for grovellers, those who'd had the sun in their eyes. I'd arrive at the big square.

The usual people were there. Couples. Mamas. Kids. I had nothing to do with them. A broken relationship. I'd go over to a street vendor. I'd buy a few seeds. I scattered them around. Pigeons would surround me. They'd peck away. I'd laugh and would imitate their cooing. I wanted to be on time for the day when God would finally notice his error: as a Bird, I'd have found my place.

◆

That afternoon, I stay in my room to turn over these memories. I tell myself that my life is a weeping sun, a sun with tears that fall like a bad rain and decompose my soul. Deadly shudders run through me.

I'm shivering. One must straddle the abyss of oblivion in order to survive. TAKE DRASTIC ACTION. Cut them off. Kick hard at the family as if at an anthill and exult as you watch the ants scatter.

Nourished by this resolution, a new one, yet another one, I get dressed. I go out into the street, my head high, chest out. I'm heading for Hassan. I whistle to myself and twirl my bag, the way the girls with the air-conditioned blacks do when they go out to the wealthy part of town, whose overbearing ease and inane behaviour I had always admired. These girls locked inside their universe of comfort, money and sophisticated laughter. I'm whistling under my breath. I tell myself I'm happy in spite of my heavy heart and the tightness in my throat. I run across neighbours. I greet them. A motion of the head. Another of the hand. I want to put an end to my body's vomiting. Happiness to ensure survival. And my gestures, every one of my gestures, speak of mountains in my heart, of trembling in my loins. To be the accomplice of the bright and luminous flesh in the shadow of the earth, one has to want it. I want it.

An improvised stadium. Two bottomless buckets attached to poles on either side of the field. Young people playing basketball. Sounds of a whistle. Comments. Cries. 'It's mine, Essomba!' 'Get the ball, Jules!' 'Ten – five!' Dribbling. Hands clapping. I stop. Their joy anoints me with salves and spices. Be happy, Tanga. Happiness is not only reserved for others. Grab it where you find it. Dive deep into happiness. Float in the blazing wave of day. Promise unhappiness, it won't be forgotten. Its sad look. Its dirty mouth. And its fingers that shred everything that moves. Tell heaven that you won't forget your comrades in Iningué, with whom you lived death to the point of laughing. Now that you have suffered, you know that suffering is a light that is lived in the dark.

An idea crosses my mind. I open my bag. I fill it with their joys, their laughter. From now on, I shall be happy. I'm holding happiness hostage.

A scratch at the bottom of my skirt. I catch hold of the fabric. I shake it. To make the bug fall off. My eyes meet a hazel gaze. Footwreck.

'What're you doing here?'

73

'I want to talk to you, Gâ.'

'You've got some nerve after what happened this morning!'

'You want me to ask your forgiveness on my knees, eh!'

'Done. Now get out!'

'I want to talk to you,' he insists.

His voice is heart-rending. I look at his face. He resembles someone who's given up waiting. His eyes are looking inwards, into himself; they're sad.

'We've said everything there is to say already.'

'Not everything.'

'Speak.'

'Come with me.'

I follow him, curiosity at my heels. He takes me into an abandoned shed. I slide in behind him. I have the feeling that I'm doing something wrong. I feel I'm on the wrong side of the law. I sit down on a stack of straw, far away from him. He lights a cigarette. I glance at the falling dusk. He takes a drag:

'Were you serious this morning?'

'As sure as I was born.'

'Nobody ever wanted anything to do with me.'

'But me, I do.'

'You don't know what you're saying.'

'I want you to become my child. I want to raise you, take you to school, fix your *pépé* soup for you, iron your clothes. I want to teach you how to believe in Santa Claus.'

'Kids' stuff. I don't believe that any more.'

'With me, it'll happen. We'll belong to every church, every religion, God will see us everywhere – he'll be obliged to see us – and Santa Claus will come.'

As I'm talking, faith comes to me bit by bit. To kill unhappiness. To violate it. To steal it. To plunder it. To capture the shade without weakening it and subject it to the torch of the seasons, the one that holds pigments – all made possible by laughter. But why doesn't the happiness in my bag react?

'I'm going to tune the violins of love,' I say. 'We'll be together, always. I'll call up the sun and place it in your eyes.'

74

I get up, go to him and I stroke his hair. He moves away. He draws a circle on the ground with his feet.

'I think you're nuts, completely nuts. Paying attention to someone like me? What an idea!'

'Why don't you let me decide that?'

'You're crazy, completely crazy, like my mother, like my father. Anyway I haven't got one. So much the better. One less madman to deal with.'

He falls silent. Short pauses. His eyes wander off, far, far away. In this time of social disintegration even children are given to reflection.

'Perhaps you're just taking me on to ensure yourself some security for your old age?'

'No, Mala.'

'D'you swear?'

'I swear it.'

'You'll never ever leave me, even if happiness were to make you senile?'

'Happiness doesn't make you senile.'

'Yes it does. It makes everybody rush about. Just look around you, Gâ, it makes everyone crazy. No more child. No more mama. No more papa. Nothing but the hope of happiness, which is an accident of nature.'

These words stop me short. Badly drawn curtains appear in my memory. Only one meagre ray of light comes through.

'You're just talking.'

'I'm telling the truth. Everyone has gone senile because of happiness. You don't need to be very bright to put together things that aren't all there. The other day I went to the movies. A Hindu film with lots of dead folk. I like the dead. At least everything is quiet, like in heaven. A woman is running around trying to find her guy that she'd lost. She falls into his arms and she cries. She says: 'I'm happy . . . I'm so happy'. Tears come to my eyes just thinking about it. And then the woman cries at the end because they've killed her guy, though she can now stick him in a hole and have him all to herself. D'you think that's normal?'

I don't respond right away. I let my brain run in slow motion, move along in a dream, then say:

'You've lost your head, my poor child. That must be your father's blood in you since no one knows who he is.'

'My father, my father. Me – I'm nobody's child. I'll even show you I'm right. Foot-wreck is always right. The other day, Djana the madman wanted to teach me how to read and write. I sat down next to him just for a laugh as usual, and because at least with him you can make fun of happiness. Then he starts telling me that the earth is round and turns around itself. And I said to myself that's why everybody is senile. Grown-ups more than children because they're set in their ways and there's nothing anyone can do for them any more. I can truly swear to you, by God, that on the one hand I refuse to grow up because of this sickness of mine, but on the other, I tell myself it's better to grow up – because at least if you fall there are the very smallest ones who can serve as your mattress.'

I close my eyes. I refuse to give a shape to his voice. I dust my clothes off. I go towards the light. He calls to me.

'You don't want anything more to do with me, do you? I knew you were speaking out of both sides of your mouth . . . Like happiness itself.'

I don't reply. I move away, covered by the murkiness that surrounds me, searching in vain for the stars to spangle the silk of my nights.

I stopped at a bakery. I ate several chocolate eclairs. I hate them. I've hurt the child. I'm gorging myself. I'm eating life to punish myself. I go to the toilet. I stick a finger down my throat. I throw up.

◆

A coughing fit suddenly cuts off the flow of the story. With her eyes bulging and covering her mouth with the palm of her hand, Tanga tries to contain her panting as she breathes. Yet again life attempts to be lived as it slips away on the quiet. She's changing form, moving on to different paths, feeling her way, pushing spectres aside, judicious, as death spreads out its sheets. Sometimes to the left, sometimes to the right, but never really present, she's always

76

searching for, mentioning, the same thing – the potential breath of the Story.

In the dim light of the candles, Anna-Claude tries to hold her back. Only the tremors of her body convey her concern as she faces the arrival of the inescapable: death. She tells herself she'll know how to obstruct it, forbid it to be in such a hurry as she works out the framework of words. Words to untie the knots, to loosen and activate the human machinery.

'I forbid you to die, you hear me? I forbid it.'

The dying woman shows a faint smile, one of those that unburdens and liberates.

'Your people knew how to define everything, prevent everything, except for that.'

'Leave my people out of it.'

'You're part of them – nothing you can do about that.'

'Yes I can. I live, I am, I can choose.'

'That's what we think, but . . .'

'What, woman?'

'In my country, each woman is not called Madame and each man is not Monsieur. What about in yours?'

'Take a guess.'

'I don't know. All I've ever seen are postcards.'

'What do they say?'

'That Christ stopped in the North.'

'And Man?'

Tanga doesn't answer. Memory, the traitor, raises its knife and lays it out across her mouth while her hand takes Anna-Claude's once more – that hand which gives and takes and which comes back to bring her some warmth in her final hour. And once again, the Story came to readjust the night with its harrows and roses.

◆

When I arrive at the appointed place, Hassan isn't there. The café where we are meeting is empty on account of this lateness. I go in and sit down, already sealed up inside myself. Nevertheless, around me the bar is enjoying its finest hour. An orchestra squeals on the beat of a cha-cha-cha. United in their love of vice, some men are eating peanuts, chomping on hard-boiled eggs, watering themselves with mugs full of beer which they empty in one gulp. And then there is Camilla, your sister, here. A white woman lost in the middle of African desires. I can't not tell you about her. Her very straight nose. Her very fine mouth. Her long legs that take her from table to table, distributing smiles and kisses. And, just as on every other night, they're on patrol those long legs of Camilla, your sister. They're on patrol and they divide themselves into thousands of Camillas in order to serve everyone with his share of her breasts. And they're beautiful. Round. Firm. In the thoughts of the men they're stuck together. They torment them before pushing them back, gasping for breath, between her thighs.

It's not beer they're coming to drink in this café. They're coming to sample Camilla's breasts.

More than one woman making her flesh available in this neighbourhood would have liked to have been a Camilla, with big breasts in an uplift bra; those breasts pleasing to the taste of the day, coming and going year in and year out between the tables and the toilet. From time to time they disappear into the washroom, followed by a man, his hand on his fly.

Camilla's story has been written. It is a mixture of sorrow and delight from which her body emerges without any memory or past, that body in which other bodies move around without brain or memory. Camilla is the woman – yesterday's dead woman – who would have bequeathed me, girlchild-woman, her story. She is the future that has been denied me. She is the sexual vessel filled with my spoils. I know that from now on Camilla will be the screen between me and the desires of men. Let her stand before me! Let them love her! Let them forget me! For I must have the house, the garden, the magpie at the end of the meadow, and children.

All these thoughts are going through me and training me to wait. In the mirror I notice Camilla's movements, between two trips to the toilet. The beauty of her breasts almost hurts me. She is braless underneath a tightly fitting tee-shirt. She roams between the tables and bends over to give the dicks riveted on her a glimpse at their contour. She pats a hand here and there, runs somewhere else as she readjusts her skirt and throws out her chest. Sitting down there, she crosses her legs, empties a whiskey in one gulp, puts her glass down noisily and continues her tour between tables and men, making her buttocks move in a sultry dance. They rise and fall, a swing in motion, down they come again. The men applaud, yelling: 'I love you, Camilla!' 'I'm drooling over you, darling!' 'Help me to forget my wife!' 'Come here on my lap, baby!' 'Make me live, make me come alive!'

Do they even ask themselves what it is that brought her here? Do they know whether the virgin canvas of woman was ever embroidered with the green of childhood? They say that Camilla was born of alcoholic parents and that she spent her childhood being tossed about from family to family. Several families is better than none at all.

This particular evening Camilla continues her stroll between tables and toilet, looking like someone who doesn't know anything about this world except for the dance of the sexes and the dawn of anxiety. Now standing, now sitting down, Camilla is always Woman. As for me, I sometimes look at her, sometimes at the entrance where Hassan is bound to stand framed in the doorway, the silhouette of the new morning light of my life, while in the night around me the inner sounds I imagine having sensed when in his arms, begin to be heard.

◆

'Tell me, my sweet, you – you're in this profession too?'

It's Camilla. She's come to me to reconcile our destinies, to chain me to an eternity of despair. I sense it; I know it. But me, girlchild-woman, I want to belong to love from now on, with the house, the dog, the magpie at the end of the meadow, the garden, children, the man. I don't want to recognise Camilla. I lower my eyes. I shake my head. I nod denial. Yes, from now on, I shall totally fulfil myself since I belong somewhere else. She looks me over from top to bottom.

'You wouldn't have thought so!'

'It's not written on anyone's forehead.'

79

'At night every cat looks grey.'

I shove my nose deep into my glass of Coke. I'm waiting for Camilla's gesture, Camilla's word that will undress me and subject my skin to that hollow of thorns and wild weeds wherein my childhood was constructed. The seconds go by. I'm incapable of looking inside myself. Who am I? Where have my dreams gone? Get the fuck away, Camilla! Let me hide my droppings! I'm just fine, Camilla, sitting on my snot and shit. Can't you understand that?

'You don't need to be ashamed,' Camilla tells me, breaking up my interior monologue. 'I know them younger than you – barely thirteen – and they've laid more men than an old chicote.'

'I'm no whore.'

Yes! DENY IT. REFUSE IT. That's a must. Contact broken. No relationship any more. Distance yourself from the past. Be yourself. But today I know you cannot change your life just by flying off on a broom. And I could have said to her:

'*Your words, woman, are a thousand needles stuck into my space so that the soul's breath can continue to exist in Man.*'

I could have told her:

'*I'm giving you my hand, woman, my hand open underneath your armpits and there, woman, I'm going to draw up the plan for wisdom in madness.*'

I could have told her:

'*Woman, the moon goes to the moon, comes there, grows, and dies on another moon.*'

Those phrases remain encircled around my tongue. I want to undo my life. Too many misfortunes have tied it into knots. I want to iron it out, to put it in order at the end of the path that love has traced. It's useful. It's necessary. I want to be the woman who has no price, no rain, who closes her heart around her man and throws away the keys. I want to be one of those women who busy themselves with the laundry, bring song into the home, carry the moon, and to the world proclaim the rapture of the feat achieved. So I find other words, I tell of the man, Hassan. I unfold the story of an eternal passion for Camilla. Maybe she's listening, maybe she isn't. I'm making her drunk. I'm inventing details. I'm tidying up the edges. I pursue her straight into the toilet.

A man is pissing as he whistles. Another one is looking at himself in the mirror, making faces. A third is wiping his hands on his trousers. And me, I draw out my words in order to finish my story. Is she following me? No matter. I'm convincing myself as the words come falling down in dribs and drabs, washing and purifying my image. The smells of urine and mildew filter into me. They give me a fever. I have no space. I don't stay put. The child. The house. The dog. The magpie at the end of the meadow. Everything is getting mixed up. My muddle. I'm adding salt to love in the stars. You have to combat the shame of humiliation. For how long have I been monopolising the words? I couldn't say. Now we are alone. Focusing on our navels, our eyes kiss without seeing each other. The noise from the bar comes to us from afar. Laughter. Cheers. Applause. Camilla has let herself slide down the wall and I sit down next to her. Then, with her eyes lost in the distance and exhaustion on her face, she talks. She tells me of the horrors, the murders she's committed against herself. She discloses that buried past which she'd meant to unearth, to shed light on.

She had loved a man, Pierre. She'd met him in Paris. He was a student. She was a waitress in a fast food restaurant in the Latin Quarter. Work. Television. Sleep. She was bored. He was looking for the woman with the flaxen hair who would serve as his ladder while he did his social climbing. He used to come into the café. She spotted him. His fleshy lips. His black skin. His frizzy hair. The deep wrinkles that cut across his forehead. He had spoken to her right away. He had said to her: 'I'd like to live my life with you.' She'd told herself: 'I'll learn to shut away my boredom.' It was time to leave Europe ... He'd taken her with him. For five years she'd rubbed her body against his. For five years she'd been bored. He would take her. She'd be bored. She'd be thinking about the all too humid heat. The people in the street. Their enormous gestures. Their pointless laughter. She was bored. In the afternoon, wrapped in a sari, with head and feet bare she'd fall into a chaise longue underneath the veranda. It was cocktail time. The houseboy would bustle about. One glass. Another one. Again and again. She'd keep drinking. She'd get drunk. When she was saturated with alcohol, she'd stick a finger down her throat. She'd feel the acrid taste burn her insides. She'd open her mouth and vomit. Unwell, she'd drag herself to her room, to her bed. With her eyes rolled upwards and her hands and forehead damp, she'd listen to her body protesting. She'd say: 'I'm going to die'. Fear would overcome her – she'd see Paris again, she wouldn't be bored any more. Walks along the Seine. Escapades in the Latin Quarter. It all seemed wonderful to her. Every little shred of her life. Beaubourg – which she never had been able to look at without feeling sick. Pigalle. Belleville. It was a sparkling world. She'd say: 'I must leave, I must save my life'. She had stayed. Pierre had left. She remained alone with two children.

Pierre. He'd never failed her. Attentive and always there. When the moment had come for the fruit of their giddiness to blossom, he was there, holding her hand, encouraging her, pushing with her, screaming with her. One day he had announced that he was leaving on a business trip. She'd packed his bags. He'd taken her in his arms and held her very tightly. He had not come back. She'd received a letter in which Pierre announced his intention to divorce her.

'My clock was running slow,' she said, shaking her head. 'I understood too late that I loved the man, that this country was really the only place where I would be able to support myself unflinchingly until the day I die.'

Pierre's departure had crushed her. At first, unkempt and dishevelled, she'd go aimlessly into the streets and the cafés, with his photographs under her arm. Pierre. Between one drink and the next, one word and the next, she'd pour out all the clichés connected with her love. With her fingers she'd slowly stroke the eyes that looked at her defiantly, the lips that had kissed her over and over again – without any possible satisfaction she thought. She'd shake her head to free herself from images that were all too carnal and broke the decrepit waves of her life. She'd go back in time. She'd tell the story. Contemptuous. Sad. Unpredictable. She said he'd left on a whim and soon would understand the role he'd been assigned and would yield to the dictates of desire. She said he'd left to punish her, to take revenge for the nights he used to spend trying to ensnare her boredom, that soon he'd be back, broken by too many moons spent imagining the smell of her. He had not returned. She went on. Then she had no words left to speak. She had to survive.

Camilla knew how to come to an arrangement with suffering – how to come to terms with it. Confronted with its labyrinths, with the cosmic void of the absence, she'd figured out how to plant her survival plans around the tree of grief. She no longer knew how to weep; she no longer knew how to laugh. Only the flesh remained. She'd reconstructed the framework of her reason around herself. With her body weighed down with Pierre's imprint, when she happened to meet someone, she'd go into a room and on to a bed – the final stage of the encounter, chosen out of anguish. Men would pass through. She wouldn't ask them for the promise of bedazzlement – for feelings. She'd have a grip on their desire. She wanted them to leave her at the break of day, her womb ravaged, incapable of any feeling. And she'd always forge ahead, rubbing her despair against their loneliness. She'd say 'more, more'. They'd take her, discovering the warm silt receiving them until they were sated. Wild with gratitude, they'd reward her with a kiss on the neck, a bank note, a drink at the bar. As the days went on, men succumbed to her. She became a drug, and gained a reputation as monumental as the woman herself: 'With Camilla, just looking at her is almost enough to satisfy you'.

But Camilla thought of Pierre. The deserter. She said she desired him, a desire born out of boredom but desire nevertheless, and one that refused to die. She said she used to drown in the abundance of sperm each time that Pierre, panting, would empty himself in her womb. She said that, unknown to her, her body would turn into a sludge, the bottom of which . . . well, the bottom of which would feed her acrimony for man.

Today, Camilla has built herself an empire and has a steady man. A client who'd come every two weeks to claim what was his due. She'd wash him and make a fuss over him. Did I understand? The guaranteed minimum was that it be permanent. Didn't every worker have a guaranteed minimum wage? She was no exception. And there were the children. Her two children who lived with her in her room. When she was entertaining she'd load them with valium and whiskey. At seven, Paul, the older one, was already a man. He was the babysitter for his younger sister. Life is so very hard!

How many times have I heard those words? Once – a thousand times perhaps! And there was always the impression they belonged to a few implacable gods. And always they had the power to take me back to the past.

◆

When I was a child, mother old one would settle down on a mat. She'd crack her fingers, sigh, and let out: 'How hard life is!' I used to listen and I'd shiver. I would look at the deep lines in her forehead, the sagging corners of her mouth. I used to get up, take a hammer and go into the streets – the winding alleys – to break stones, the walls of trouble. All day long I'd break and pillage. I wanted the evil vibrations of life to be annihilated. I was hoping; I was hitting hard. Arches. Vaults. Cloisters. When my hands had lost every colourful possibility of finding rest, I'd come back to my mother old one, proud of myself, upheld by a silent joy I'd try to give to her. I'd question her. Was life always a stone? Yes! I'd go off again, more determined than ever, a tough woman among tough guys. I'd collect stones, gather them up in a sack and pour them out on the asphalt. A car would drive by, and another and another . . . I'd look at my stones. Intact. I'd hold my head between my hands and I'd laugh. My blood was weeping deep inside and yet I was laughing – laughing at the hardheadedness of adults who insisted on holding on to the sorrowful tonalities of the world.

That evening, though, in the washroom of the café, I would have liked to break down the wall of grief to let hope's companion into Camilla's body. But I can do nothing, I must do nothing – I am too busy tearing the veil of my own anguish. She smiles at me and tells me she'd like to be me, to give her genitals some rest, if only for one day, so that her womb might get some sleep. She says she could exist, live in a different world where men look in order to speak instead of to touch; to touch until they imprint a wound – fire – into her belly. But that's what she wanted, after all! To let them grind her down! To let them kill her! Do I think she's beautiful? I say I do.

84

She gets up immediately and lifts her dress to show me her belly covered with fine down all the way up to her breasts. Men adore that, she says, as she tugs at it and smiles to herself. I'm watching. A sudden rage grips me.

'In any event, you white people you're born clean, with happiness on your lips.'

'You're wrong.'

'Phooey!'

'Abandoned children, the unemployed, whores, battered women – they're all there in my country, too.'

'You have the government. It protects you.'

'Yes. Even from living,' she says bitterly.

'It's better than grief.'

'What do you know about it? Your people make use of the undesirables. Ours lock them up; herd them together. That's no better.'

'Yes it is.'

'D'you know what an insane asylum is, a rest home, a correction centre, an orphanage?'

'It's better than nothing!'

I'm raising my voice. She looks at me. How do I explain to her that as a child I dreamed of going to her country without any luggage, because there was Social Security for me there and even for my dog? How do I tell her she's trampling on the illusions of a child?

Before, Paris was my refuge. I'd go there on foot every time the world's absurdities grabbed hold of me. I'd call my friends. I'd hold forth about Paris – the lovely life we'd have there. Leaving for Paris is the most exquisite thing that could have happened in my goddam life. I'd even see myself as a baby, asleep in a real cradle. Sometimes, I'd clap my hands, I'd grow up for no reason other than to bite into the apple of France and some ham. Then I'd become tiny again in my cradle, with a dummy in my mouth, and I'd really smile.

I'd organise my departure for Paris like a real expedition. We'd come together on the village square, we children. A fistful of barren seeds, we were not aware then that we had no hope other than to brandish the banner of our imagination.

'We're getting the hell away from here, guys,' I'd say.

'Where're we going?'

'To Paris.'

'Again!'

'This time, guys, we're going all the way.'

'That's what you always say,' says Gal, a coward.

'Nobody's asking you to come along with us.'

'I love it,' Ningue'd lisp with his bad teeth, 'I feel like having apples.'

'What would you eat them with?' others ask, making fun of him.

'Quiet down, guys. Let's go, if we want to get there before nightfall.'

Wrapped in our rags, we divide up into groups of four or five. We go into the supermarket. Some of us distract the assistants. Others swipe some apples. We bring them back to the shed. We count them. We put them into a cardboard box. We bury it.

There's a way of going to Paris without taking a plane: you lock up its symbols in a tomb. And here's Camilla trying to create disorder in my flights into the past. I get up. I lower her dress which is still rolled up around her hips. Her eyes are looking at me; they don't understand; I kiss her neck.

'You're beautiful, Camilla.'

'Men prove it to me all the time.'

'You should have stayed in your own country.'

'And why is that?'

'You wouldn't be here dragging around, suffering.'

'Here at least I exist. You understand?'

'You'll always be out of place.'

'At least, I can invent empty spaces and fill them with life.'

'And your children?'

She was caught off guard! Her features are wasting away. She no longer looks like herself. She turns her eyes away so she can't see herself any more. She drags herself round on her behind. She grabs a broom and twists toilet paper around it. She lays it against her heart. She cradles it. She weeps.

'Sleep my baby, sleep my sweet. Mamma is coming to you. The

86

clouds will be your cradle. I'll make your bed in the clouds, there where hearts are twinkling. Sleep my child, sleep my child . . .

There are some things in life you order but for which you refuse to pay the bill. I dodge the woman's grief. I take a piece of toilet paper and wipe the rain away from her eyes. I draw back. I want to flee the horror of the scene and the blue brightness of my dress is already swinging towards the door. Camilla's laughter seizes me. Later on I will learn that her two children died in an explosion of bottled gas. I respect her for that. May God forgive me.

The crowd had become larger. They're trembling while they wait for Camilla. I glide into their desire without touching it – without attaching any pleasure to it. Hassan is there in a grey suit, absorbed in reading a newspaper. I come up close to him to the point where it might possibly be recognisable as tenderness. My eyes prickle with shards. They slash him to ribbons – his head, his hands, his feet. Ugly? Ugly. Vulgar? Vulgar. I wind up memory's clock. No coincidence. Just another man. The only thing left to love is the dream.

Is it out of boredom or despair that we paint a scene to be lived out? I refrain from weeping. My love – I want it to be strong, capable of nourishing itself. I want to live surrounded by everything that my memory builds upon the love of man. To connect the shapes from the inside and unfold them into shapes on the outside. No common sense. I want to anchor myself amidst my dreams, to raise myself up above destiny. The story must be – to challenge the disruptive elements that are unsuited to the enlightenment of the state of grace; to plunge into reverie to cross the threshold of the impossible universe. To invent.

But is that not the characteristic of the stillborn child, to be telling itself stories while fornicating? What's to be done in a country where the adults, unable to resist the suggestions of misery, have abolished reality's space?

I put my desires back to where they were – the time and place that I first met Hassan. I moisten my lips. I straighten my skirt. 'Hi!' I say as I plant a kiss on his mouth.

He looks up without answering. His forehead is tight. I know – I the girlchild-woman used to the whims of men, to their bad moods where it concerns a woman who is failing in her duty to be submissive – I know, just by looking at his hard expression, I know that a storm is brewing very close to us. The moment to transgress laws, to draw the sword of my defense is now or never.

'What's the matter with you? Aren't you pleased to see me?'

'Sure. But . . .'

'But what?'

He fiddles with the newspaper, rubs the tablecloth.

'I've been here for half an hour waiting for you.'

'My mind has been looking for you for more than twenty-four hours, did you ever think of that?'

Then I say: 'I love you. Since I love you, talk to me about me.'

I pull up a chair to sit down and allow my hearing the time needed to listen and imprint some elation on to my memory's printing plate. I take out a cigarette. I pin it between my lips. Hassan rushes to give me a light. I send puffs of smoke in his direction.

'So?' I say.

'I don't like to be kept waiting.'

'Stop right there. That's all you've ever done since you were born. Like everybody else. Wait! Wait! And time is always the one who wins the race. You have to . . .'

The words get stuck in my mouth with Camilla's entrance. Our eyes meet. They rub against each other – they go on and on and resound in me. My thoughts cave in. My nerves break down as well. I want to move beyond her. My agitated senses bring me back to her, to our eyes that are there like a curtain hung between two half-open doors. Doubt plagues me: I fear this look is opening them wide, mixing us together, revealing me.

'You know her?' Hassan questions me as he turns his eyes to Camilla.

'No.'

'So much the better. I hate women who make an exhibition of their ass.'

He gets up, folds his paper, and pulls us – me and my lie – out of the café.

The night welcomes us – humid and like an accomplice. I don't resist its sepulchral depths. I want to bury my lie underneath a pile of stones and take on its posture and its situation as I await the wedding of deliverance. I want to place my feet carefully so as not to ring the carillons of the past. I want to speak wordlessly, to pin down with muddy soles those caresses when my body has offered itself to feed mother old one. I want to spread the seeds of immortality so that all the past becomes tied to it and untied before it's torn up.

But being disillusioned with existence is the most solitary and the most tenacious of human flaws. It empties the body of all joy and kills any feeling of hope or whatever might resemble it. It allows it to return to the mortuary territories of bones before sculpting hatred into it.

Happiness, where are you?

I tell myself: 'Tanga. If you've reached this point it's the old ones who are to blame. It's their fault if you've been condemned to the dirt.'

And there, by Hassan's side, hatred arrived. With small strokes at first. I'm relearning my first anger. My heart becomes sharp as a harpoon. My flesh gets tense. A chronic illness – I recognise its symptoms. Evil approaches. In red. In black. In grey. Always the same, tailor-made for me. It penetrates me, drives its spear into me, strips me bare. I no longer recognise myself. However much I try to control myself, I can't prevent myself from seeking out the facts that are poisoning and killing me. I am becoming the demented scorpion related to the darkness. The quest of evil – always the quest of evil. It gives me my memory. Images parade before my eyes. The past attacks me, always the past.

◆

I am six years old. Sun. Humidity. I'm trotting along at father old one's side. I'm hurrying to adjust myself to his height. He's taking me to his mistress-woman, the fish vendor. As soon as she sees us, she comes towards father old one, her bare torso shining with palm oil, the curve of her back accentuated, her hips supple. She takes his hand and puts it on her breasts. He looks her up and down. With his eyes like torches, he kisses her, and says: 'You chase the dusk away, I feel myself getting younger again.' She laughs, claps her hands and makes her bracelets jingle. She looks down at me, strokes my hair, hands me a balloon and pulls father old one to the bed, which shortly begins to creak underneath their weight.

How can I describe the arrow that pierces and then buries me? How do I put a name to it? Jealousy, no doubt. But hatred above all; loathing of what moves and brings emotion ... Death to the entire family!

I curl up in a corner. I stop up my ears against the weeping bed, against the mounting sounds of heavy breathing. I don't want to see anything; I don't want to hear anything. I blow into the balloon. It swells and swells. I tell myself it's like the belly of a woman expecting a baby. I bite into it. It bursts. Father old one jumps up and turns round to me.

'What's going on?'

His fear makes me laugh. He lets go of his companion. He leaps to my side. He slaps me. My eyes are blurred with tears. My laughter swells up. What does my real state matter? In his rush, father old one forgot to pull up his trousers. He stumbles on his way back to the fish vendor. With his shoulders contracted and his buttocks pinched together, he hobbles forward and drops down on the bed. My laughter breaks off. I curl up in my corner – the child's place.

How do you live in a country that goes along upside down? Turn towards the sky? It remains obstinately silent. The men get drunk on jojoba and do their utmost to blaspheme against a forgetful God. Prisoners caught within the barbed wire of tradition, the women roam around the muck-filled streets, forever and always following the sex organs that tear them to pieces. As for the children, they let death take them away, grown old from having pounded too many manioc leaves to feed their parents.

I jump. Hassan's arm is clinched around my waist. His voice brings me back to reality.

'Shall we go to the hotel?' he murmurs into the hollow of my neck.

'No!'

'You don't like being with me?'

'Yes I do. But you have to learn about desire in absence.'

'I want you, little one,' he says as he takes me in his arms.

90

'Leave me alone. I am nobody's little one.'

'Well then, go to hell! I wonder if you even know how to love, if your cunt hasn't become blunted together with your common sense.'

I shrug my shoulders. He moves away. I stay on the corner of the street. I lean up against a wall and sniff hard in order not to start sobbing. With my face in my hands, I'm in a blue funk for remaining behind without him – without anyone. I call out his name. He doesn't look back. I wipe away the snot hanging from my nose and I run after him.

A hotel room. Walls covered in oxblood red. At the back, a wardrobe with a mirror whose edges show rust. On the floor, a worn carpet decorated with pink-fleshed dancers. In the middle, a double bed with a bedside light on either side. One of them, in frosted glass plate, lets through a softened light. The other one is broken, its lampshade replaced with a black metal plate riddled with luminous holes.

Hassan bolts the door. He takes me in his arms. I push him away.

'Talk to me.'

'You're not going to start your nonsense again, are you? You're forgetting that in a few years you'll be worth nothing any more. Your breasts, your behind, your belly, it's all going to be sagging. Take advantage of the here and now. Everything has its time and place. That's the way of the wise.'

'I don't give a damn if I grow old. And I'm fed up with meeting people who're lugging the city, the village, and the bag of their ancestors' bones around on their back. All of them are the living dead. Where are the truths? What would it be like if the sun weren't to rise in the East or if straw were to weigh more than stone?'

'Listen, old girl, I've got enough problems of that sort. And when I'm with a pretty girl, it's something totally different I want.'

'To split open my genitals, of course?'

'No, to love them. But you, women, you're like the wind. You pass through and leave us alone with our anxieties.'

'You think I'm a woman?'

'I don't know. But you are desirable, that you are. That ought to be enough for you.'

'No!'

'I've got nothing else to offer you.'

'Yes you do. Your love.'

'It's broken. In the past, I used to feel, I used to suffer, I used to

92

be alive. A woman came into my life and she left. I'll say it again, I've nothing else to offer you.'

'Give me a chance.'

'A chance. What for?'

I don't reply. How can I tell him about the house, the dog, the garden, the magpie at the end of the meadow, the man, children? How can I explain to him that the cracks in him represent my survival and that I'm prepared to glue the bits and pieces of his being back together again so that they'll fit perfectly? I sigh and let myself fall back on the bed. I'm waiting for him to possess me. He sinks down on my breasts. He kisses my eyelids. Why these gestures of tenderness if I'm nothing but a piece of meat? He says he's submerged in bedroom fantasies, and that my almost hairless genitals are fanning his desire. I remain silent. He says he's going to mould me as a sculpture into his desires and that from now on I will insist on techniques from other men that he will have taught me. I remain silent. He gets up, takes a razor out of his pocket and gets started on my pubic hair, what little I have. I do not move. I leave my basin of flesh in his fingers and let him shape other images of me. He stops, contemplates his work, sends compliments in my direction in a low voice before he collapses on top of me again and rips into my sex with one rough thrust.

Not a cry comes from my throat. Only the sounds of the night inhabit me. Laughter. Snatches of conversation. A balaphon in the distance. Pounding. He lets go of me, rolls over on his back, out of breath. I get up to leave him. He holds me back and pulls me close to him:

'What's the matter with you?'

'I want to shut off my memory. It's persecuting me.'

'You really are difficult. Anyway, women today are nothing but a sack full of problems. And they call that LIBERATION,' he adds sarcastically.

'If you married me, I'd have no problems any more.'

'Marry you? But you're totally nuts, old girl! Do you know what would happen to you? You'd lose your beauty. Like all the others.'

And to discourage me, he evokes images of matrons sitting underneath verandas with their flabby bellies. He tells of their sagging breasts, the sour voice of the disappointed spouse which little by little goes altogether mute. Not even any tears to weep over the lack of pleasure! No more sex! Violated by the husband on the wedding day! Is that what I expect from life? I do not reply. I get up. My body is without strength, pulverised by the thumbscrews of despair. I put on my sandals. I scrutinise the blackish stain on the sheet, the results of our revels. I turn on my heels towards the door, towards the street. Hassan doesn't hold me back. I never saw him again.

◆

Hope strangled in its shell. Black night. I don't remember the names of the alleys I wandered through very well. But I do know that despair had the stink of an icecold desert that night.

I played at being a car in the street. I ran along, fists tightened, as if I was going to run everyone over. I knocked some drunks over. They hissed after me: 'Whore's daughter!' 'Slut! Vermin!' They stank, enough to make you vomit, like their hair. A streetkid stepped in my way. He obstructed my passage. I spat in his face before running off as fast as I could. I'm hot. The evening's cool wind glues my clothes to my skin. In the velvet of the night I feel like I'm lightweight, ethereal, almost a shadow. I want to witness the body's endangering of the body. To destroy. To pillage. I call upon the explosion that will bring annihilation. That will trample everything so as to have only the idea of life. I stopped in front of a gate. A nightwatchman. I approach him. He's sleeping with his face towards the sky and his mouth open. I want to talk to him. That or something else . . . I step over him; I go away; I come back; I pretend to be looking for something lost. I come by again. I jostle him. He wakes up with a start.

'Is there a thief?' he asks as he scratches his testicles.

I tell him no, but that we could be associates and make a nice deal together. He wakes up fully now.

'What'you want, girl?'

'Some business, man.'

'What sort?'

'Furniture removal.'

'Explain.'

'We could move your boss for example. Nobody would ever suspect you.'

I hardly have time to get these words out when he lets loose in an animal-like explosion. I pick up the hem of my dress and run off as fast as I can down the street. An arrow whistles past my ears and ricochets on the asphalt. He's shouting: 'Dirty whore! Thief! Scum! Crazy woman! Next time I'll drill holes all over your ass!' I ran until I felt my heart give out. I saw a gutter. I took a piss, whimpering with joy. I've just made myself useful: the nightwatchman will receive a bonus.

◆

When I arrive home, mother old one is there, in a crumpled heap on the mat with a cap on her head to protect her from father old one's ghost. The elderly members of the family are around her. They're all here – shabby, doddering, weighing heavily upon time without end, their frames shrunken. Here they all are jerking their carcasses around, spitting out proverbs. They're all here – cousins, second cousins, third cousins of Kadjaba Dongo, my grandmother. One-eyed Médé. Essoumba, the paralytic. Wolvegang, the carpenter. And their wives at their left. Others as well. All the senile old people of Iningué, distilling death, squatting on their bits of matting. As soon as they see me, they straighten up their bones, raise their sepulchral faces up to me and call in unison:

'There she is!'

I float into the room with my spirit frozen and my body in pain. They order me to sit down for the great family council that has gathered to examine my case. I pull up a chair and drop down on it, my gaze riveted to the floor. The most ill-humoured one, who forgets so much that he no longer has any age, limps over to me with his cane in his hand. From his toothless jaws I get the full blast of his decaying breath in my nostrils.

'*Youuuuyouu!*' he thunders.

He thumps the floor three times with his foot, raises his cane,

95

invokes the spirit of the ancestors to silence everyone. A few more whispers. A fart. A belch. Then there is calm.

'My dear brothers. We are here tonight to put some reason into this child's head.'

'Mmmmm,' the others agree shaking their heads.

'Thank you father,' mother old one says as she wipes her nose.

'The child wants to starve us to death, while we put life itself into her mouth. Even our dead will not accept this.'

'Mmmmm,' the crowd agrees more emphatically.

'We want justice!'

'Mmmmm.'

'If God created her body to look like this, it's so that it will be of use. And it must stay with us all the way to the final hole.'

'*Ywééééé*!' the crowd screams, suddenly excited.

I don't want to hear anything else; I cannot take any more time to listen to this. I run off to my room. The girl my sister hasn't come home yet. I double lock the door behind me.

'Open up! Open up!' they command as they bang on the door.

No corpse is more mute nor more rigid than I am. I'm putting myself outside the circle of their control, their laws. They knock, they shout, they yell. They say some day I'll perish in a gutter and neither vultures nor hyenas will want any part of my dead body. I remain silent. They say my womb will rot away before dusk and my children will be cursed with silence. They squeal, swarm, let out ghastly things, these people flayed by death. I open my handbag, take out a banknote of a thousand francs, slide it underneath the door. A great silence. One after the other I hear them packing up. And mother old one's whining litany: 'I told you, I told you! This child was born from a drought!'

I let myself drop back on my bed. I light a cigarette and play with the cloud of smoke that falls across my eyes. The idea that I might be able to drown my past in it shoots through me. Father old one, he used to bury his present. His look was a stare. He thought that the origin of all life was an illusion. Eating and drinking were illusions. He excelled in this. He'd tell himself stories, jigsaw puzzle stories wherein he was the architect, roadbuilder, foreman of the construction site. When he wasn't chasing skirts, he had himself photographed, dressed in bell-bottom trousers, a checkered jacket, and his eyes hidden behind enormous Ray-Bans made in Macao. He was becoming immortal. Today in front of the Eiffel Tower, tomorrow on the Champs-Elysées, yesterday in front of the Madeleine. Papier-mâché monuments, as atrophied as Iningué itself. He'd send the photos to the village in pink envelopes, the words 'For those who remained in the village, guardians of tradition' written on the back in clumsy handwriting. Nervous at heart, he'd turn to mother old one and bray: 'Me, I have really made a success of my life. How envious they must be!' He'd shiver and give his face a moment to look lighthearted and happy. Mother old one would nod her head, smile, and go back to what she was doing.

In my country, the past is locked away, the future too. Identity has stopped at the boundary between yesterday and today. Sometimes I write to heaven to ask it for the recipe for laughter.

◆

When I was younger, I was envious of cops. They represented the strength that would allow me to struggle against decay and find my way back to the stars. I dreamed of cops. The blows of their sticks, the excitement of shadowing someone, the sunshine of their gold braid. Just like in the movies when they enter and kill the bad guy. Then one day, the cops came. The universe fell apart. After that I learned that dogs and wolves look alike at night.

So I searched elsewhere. I snooped around the earth to try to understand. I spent my birthdays looking for words that illuminate – going down their chasms, climbing up their peaks. Nothing. Always nothing. Not even any walls to stop the heat. Then there was this man, Kamgué. I was twelve seasons old. He was sixteen. He taught me some words: Injustice. Poverty. Oppression. I'd listen; I'd suffer. We went into the streets together, stones in hand with an army of children in rags behind us. Shop windows would fly as we passed. Tyres burned. Adults would flee and hide behind the lowered shutters of stores. We were shrieking: 'Millet! Millet!'

Silences were born from the noise of our stones. Dense silences. Putrid. Unhealthy. The cops came looking for my friend. They murdered him and made it look like suicide. Faced with the horror, some were getting ready to vomit their disgust, but the silence of the guns disappeared inside them. The others – all the others – kept their lips sealed. So as not to be tempted to speak and to see, they played ostrich. Nothing seen. Nothing heard. Not even the smoke and barking of the rifles.

◆

The sub-prefect called for father old one.

I remember. An ashen day. Rain and wind. Cursed day! Fog. Flooding. In the streets, the jangling of empty bottles, the din of sheet metal ripped off by the storm, the rolling sound of tin cans. The wind twists the mango trees, scatters leaves and branches across the water, torn off by death in her haste. Mother old one keeps herself busy with a yam. My father, just back from his interview, walks on tiptoe. He sighs. He snorts. He gesticulates. Judging by his jerky movements, I'm already swimming in the flood of insults that are going to swallow me up. I curl up in a corner. Become an obstacle. Wait for the moment when his words are going to nail me to the silence of obligatory respect.

In the middle of the night, speech is still missing and I'm beginning to hope for the exonerating silence in which the soul ascends to heaven without ever even lightly brushing against purgatory. I let go of my anxieties. I'm already climbing the steps of hope when mother old one shoots over to me. She's disgusted, sick to her stomach:

'Ah!. . . Wretched girl. How dare you? Eh, tell me? Why?'

Violence unfurls. I protect my face. The first smack comes, followed by a volley of blows. I lie down. I play dead. She pounces upon me, crushing me. She strikes and invokes her labour pains, her forgotten woman's body, the *pagne* she didn't buy, taxes. Father old one understands, he sees. He understands just from the revelation of her fury alone that he's guilty of an outrage against my mother the woman and that my being punished is payment for his mistake.

Isn't that justice? He'd given me up to her without any reservations, without any restrictions, heaven knew that. It was proper that I should serve as scapegoat for the household's ill temper. And father old one sinks into his easy chair, his nerves frozen in the rumination of things it would be better not to hear. When she's exhausted herself beating me, mother old one pulls herself together and collapses on her mat. I remain vacant, enclosed in my pain. Father old one chooses this moment to pull himself up out of his chair and stand rooted in front of me.

He says: 'Nothing must change. In the name of the ancestors, that is my command!'

Mother old one concurred.

He says: 'The child must not budge. Respect alone must breathe.'

Mother old one concurred again.

He says: 'The child is very lucky. When I was eight years old, I was in the street, with a bare torso, always bent under the weight of loads of bananas. Every day, in the dry season when the earth is cracked as well as in the rainy season when the sky becomes a torrential flood.'

'The child is lucky,' he repeated. 'It can go out and play, watch legs in the stores when it gets bored. That should be sufficient – that has to be sufficient.'

Mother old one jumped up from her mat to pull his boots off.

And I, the child, I looked no further. I didn't want to see that ghastly thing any more – my friend's body hacked to pieces. I didn't want to hear a thing any more, ashamed to have been the only girl in Iningué to shout about hunger in the streets. I decided to wash away the error by crouching before the void's cavern, to embroider the tablecloth of the absurd bequeathed to me by my parents.

◆

That night, after the scene with the old people, I spend a long time cloaking myself in memories, pushing a dagger into my scalp to ransack the germ that has begotten me. From time to time I drop off into a strange half-sleep. A forest of thorns welcomes me. I'm fascinated. I penetrate into its bowels. These become transformed into thousands of aggressive old men. They're toothless. They stink. They're crippled. I back away. They proclaim themselves to be the fingers of Providence. They encircle me. They strangle me. I extricate

99

myself. I howl. Their grip tightens. At the moment of the final spasm, I wake up with a start. I've soiled my bed.

◆

'The world can perish,' Anna-Claude says, interrupting the Story's rolling wave! 'It can perish with its mouth wide open, I won't lift another finger.'

'Take it easy.'

'Take it easy? You don't understand, you just don't understand,' she says as she jumps up. 'I've been working for a long time, collecting money so that not one child in the world would ever go hungry again. Today, I realise it's just another come-on.'

Anna-Claude. She'd built her life on a monument of wind. Day after day she had asked her dream for help, for the solace of its voice ... A tremendous delusion that had nurtured her, caressed her, cajoled her, over and over again, from the day her schoolmates had excluded her from their games, calling her a dirty Jew. She didn't understand – she the creature of day, the light in sorrow's imprint. With heart torn apart, she had gone home and asked her mother to wash her, to find a brand of detergent that would whiten the tee-shirt of her skin better than it did yesterday, and would allow her to enter into complicity with the others. The next day, she'd returned to school, full of cleanliness, blighted in her whiteness. She approached a group of children involved in a game of marbles. Shy, but spick and span, she opened her hands. Her mouth grew wide with feeling.

'Look,' she said, 'I'm all clean.'

They stopped playing and their eyes met in a conspiracy. They began to talk very softly. She didn't understand what they were saying but she knew the Geneva Conference was in session, and after a quick tour round the table the laughter took off. Taunting. Thunderous. It came raining down from everywhere. She lowered her head to open channels in her body so the sediment her life was burdened with could flow away. She waited, hoping for the dawn to come that would take her out of semi-darkness. The day had not arrived.

100

They had formed a circle around her. They took it in turns to kick her to the beat of their 'Dirty Jew!' Traces of tears and snot were covering her face, hollowing out a network of hatred in her memory. How many blows did she receive? She couldn't say. Judgement no longer existed. She had nothing but her tears to describe their darkness to a race of children who were widowers of love, ready to jab their feet into her ass, thereby awakening the travelling recluse in her.

From that day on, she learned not to be Jewish any more, not to be any more, to clothe herself in dreams and thereby to kill he anguish. Hour after hour she'd lay the foundations of the imagination. Stone by stone . . . On the brink of herself. She slipped away from the insults, from the alibi of tension which justified the stroke of the knife. She stood very straight behind the partition of hell. After her teacher, whose flesh was crawling with fear, sent her away from school and when her mother, bogged down in her distress, wept over the cursed and tormented children, over the star that would puncture them from now on, Anna-Claude, convulsed with joy, went over to her and said:

'Don't cry, mamma. It's the star of the heart.'

◆

As an adolescent she went through books compulsively. She did research on those people who had not invented gunpowder; the blockhead who had not distilled the cannon's blast; the one that resists madness and does not turn out sententious theories sitting behind a table; the one that does not take pride in knowing the multitude of degradations. She headed for that place where man strides through the streets without doing a survey of them first, where man resembles Man. She found Ousmane's people. She decided that she belonged to them, that her man with the thick-set beard bore that name, that she would know ecstasy's thrill after all the destruction and debris. Today her life is falling apart. Ousmane's people DO NOT EXIST. What she found was a people that knows how to inflict death despite their ante-diluvian weaponry. A people that knows how to count monsters and make their horns grow against

101

terror. Goldsmiths of cruelty, they carry their gangrenous affliction in their hands.

How do you explain all that to the dying woman? How do you tell her of the dream that gets away, that leaves without achieving its mission: to put the being to sleep. Because as long as human beings sleep, beauty belongs to this world. There's nothing to be said, other than to let herself be enveloped by the dying woman and allow the Story to reveal her body, the widow of joy.

◆

It's after four o'clock the following day when I make up my mind to leave the room. The girl my sister is there, in her skimpy dress showing off her chest. She's dozing with spittle at the corners of her mouth after her first night of business. I work my way around her without making any noise, for I know – I girlchild-woman, used to the dance of the sexes – I know that these repulsive nights are long and that the days have to be spent tracing sleep's silhouette . . . I find a *pagne*. I cover her legs and go out into the daylight.

It's the hour when siesta time's gossip erupts. It unfurls the tongues of women who sit in groups of four or five underneath the mango trees, on the verandas and in front of the bars. Loves. Hates. Disappointments. Those little things that add spice to life, shed light on it in a hundred different ways, and unite people in their universal mediocrity.

I walk on in the sleepy sun. I walk as if out of joint, rigid in my distress. In front of me the cemetery cordons off its silence. I open the gate, distraught with grief. I wander between the graves, placed between mankind and the stars, when suddenly I spot a tomb of beaten earth, covered with brambles sweeping back and forth in the fingers of the wind. A small cross. An inscription:

> Jean-Marie Diop
> 20 October 1960 – 4 March 1978
> Died on the battlefield

Still a child, buried deep underneath earth's feet.

I crouch down. I pick up a lump of clay encrusted with gravel. I

102

hide it inside my vagina. Mother old one's face appears before me. My brain is draining. Goodbye, Ma. I'll come back. To train myself in being cursed so that not one perilous leap can escape me. I'm concealing a viper inside my vagina. It will distil the poison. It will envenom anyone who gest lost in there. I'm brandishing my redis-covered virginity for humanity. I'm singing. Yes, Ma, I'm singing, with the scourge of existence all around me like a halo. How much time went by while I was in this delirium? I couldn't say. Time had left my spirit. Every minute brought forth its plans for flight, slowly, very slowly, second after second until insanity displayed itself. I hoisted myself up on the tomb, I touched heaven. I heard the first call of the last birds. I climaxed, with the conviction that only dread gave access to the world's realities.

I rub my eyes. Several times. I mustn't let myself be carried off by the river of my own anguish. I have left the dead behind.

I go down the street, taking detours so as not to run into familiar faces. Superstition. I take an alley here, a path there. I go down a slope and arrive at the shed where Mala and I saw each other the night before. He is there. He is waiting for me, upright in his tatters, a hoop in his hand. As soon as he sees me he walks to meet me with his awkward gait. I open my arms; he stops the motion that would fling him into my arms.

'What has happened to you?'

'Nothing.'

'What d'you mean, nothing! Your legs are covered with blood.'

'Phooey!'

He shrugs his shoulders. Then:

'I didn't know you were coming.'

'You don't know me very well. As time goes by you'll see.'

'It's hard to understand grown-ups. Anyhow, they're so compli-cated that they don't even understand each other any more.'

'Stop talking nonsense and follow me.'

'What do we start with?'

'I don't know.'

'Knowing is all you have to do. If you want my opinion, we should begin at the beginning and stay right there. That way nothing

103

ever changes, nothing ever moves. And everything will always be new. God ought to think the way Mala does.'

I stammer out some explanations taken from the repertory of riddles which cannot be explained. Inflicting motionlessness upon the audience with words that can go either way, as teachers do. I wrap some whys and wherefores together, clenching my hands, these hands responsible for madness, alone capable of doing or undoing, of changing black into colour.

I go into the shed. I sit down on a stone. The present is flying through my fingers and nothing but a memory in which I let myself be caught.

A child used to live here once. Dirty. Smelly. A hopping gait. For entire days, covered with earth, he'd stay in his shed talking to the rats and mice who seemed to listen to him lovingly. Sometimes, when the night prolonged the pain of his ulcers, he'd slip into the shadows with his nerves on edge. He'd go through the rubbish bins, pushing away banana and plantain peel, sifting, digging, looking for a piece of meat some man's hand had forgotten. A noise? He'd tremble and straighten up immediately. His eyes like lamps, he'd look around and then disappear into the night.

Cursed. An albino.

Mala comes closer to me, giving his steps the light puff of a breath and rests his head against my shoulder.

'You crying?'

'No.'

'Doesn't matter anyway when there's two of us.'

I smile. I draw him close to me. The child's body is warm. Moist as well. He wants a cigarette. I light one and give it to him. He smokes. I cradle him. I recall the time in the village – the dry season when the soil cracks open, the rainy season and the peanut harvest. I talk about the fire in the evening and the children around it, the crippled old woman who chews tobacco as she tells stories of owls, the village chief and his thirty wives. Then I tell him the story of the little sailor who had built a garden on the edge of the sea. I repeat it – it's the only one I know. And before going to sleep, he saw the sailor burying his goldfish several times and watering it to make it grow. I lay him down on a bundle of straw. I get up. I mustn't disturb his sleep.

I lift my *pagne* high up over my thighs and I urinate around him. I trample the flow of my body three times. I spit abundantly. I have just marked the outline of my territory. I cover him with a piece of cardboard and leave the place on tiptoe.

When Foot-wreck wakes up, I am crouching by his bedside, a piece of cake in my hands.

'You want to taste?'

'I don't want to pick up habits like that – that way I am not taking any chances.'

'Still, we'll have to see each other often now – every day. We should come back tomorrow.'

'Don't know if I have time for all this fuss and bother, but if this sort of thing means a lot to you . . .'

'Learn to obey!'

My tone is dry. I feel like a queen – I give orders. I direct. I ennoble. Foot-wreck looks up at me with glowering eyes. I laugh. I'm bewildering to him. I want to express the strident prayer of love that only a gesture can gratify. I lean over to him. I kiss him on the cheek, on his forehead. I give him the cake. He wavers.

'Take it. I brought it for you.'

He takes it, wraps it up in an old newspaper and then stuffs it in his pocket.

'Aren't you going to eat it?'

'No, not now. I'm not hungry during the day. That's for little kids.'

'But you're my kid!'

'I'm nobody's kid. And if you want to be my mother, you'll have to start right back at the beginning, otherwise it's tacky.'

His voice dwindles. The tears he tried to control escape from his eyes. I open my blouse. I bend down so that his mouth is at the level of my breasts. I force his lips open. He's breathing hard, snorting. I insist, he gives in and suckles, slowly, very slowly. His eyes are disturbed as if they were jutting out over a ravine and it might be better to watch out for the wedding of heaven and earth.

Later I learned he'd saved the cake for his grandmother.

Throughout the days that followed, I held on to the confused feeling of these hours of happiness. My body was at rest. The girl my sister was taking my place with Monsieur John and rather successfully so, to judge by her bursts of laughter when the foul old man took her between his knees, drenching her with his vanilla scent gone sour, and lisped in a sugary voice: 'Let me see your pretty little titties. Come on now, be nice.'

Monsieur John was pleased with the change. Young flesh. He came three times a week, dripping in his suit, long-sightedness behind his lecherous little eyes. He'd stop in front of me, breathing heavily and bobbing up and down from one foot to the other. He'd come out with a hurried 'How're you?' and then ask me where my sister was. I would merely point to the place where she could be found. He'd go in; he'd leave; the cash stayed.

Mother old one was sullen with me. I was playing the game of love and complete indifference with her. I devoted myself to this to kill her passion for gain. Cash is tenacious! A depraved infatuation which caused her to be mistrustful of everything. At first, she used to bury her savings in shithouses. Nobody could go in without her sticking her face up to the keyhole to spy on them. No more danger! When they came out, she would ask with a perverse smile: 'You didn't find anything in there?'

'Such as what, Ma?'

'Oh nothing, nothing ... Sometimes there are things on the ground.'

But for the love of her life, shithouses were still too exposed. After that she would carry her banknotes on her body, in her underwear. Menstruation time? Yes, her period came. She lost her savings. Paralysed with hatred, she took advantage of each of my troughs, of each of my flaws to slither to the horizon and install the night.

◆

That particular afternoon, girdled with exhaustion, I collapsed on a rattan chair. The girl my sister is taking a siesta. Heat. Humidity. In the courtyard, huge red ants are tackling a cockroach. I watch their stratagem with the feeling of a happy death. The air is filled with a strong smell of spices and burnt oil. Sickening. Mother old one isn't there and alone, briefly, with the pleasure of being alive, I am beginning to learn what the colour of time is when I see her coming into the courtyard followed by dozens of people. Bald ones. Fat ones. Some wobbly on their legs. A whole assortment of human beings! They approach me menacingly. I straighten up. They stop right in front of me, mother old one in the lead:

'She's the one,' the old woman shrieks, 'I'm sure she's the one.'

'What, Ma? What have I done?'

'Aaaaah! . . . The nerve. She even has the gall to ask what she's done!'

The crowd snickers. Some of them whistle. Others raise their fists. A kid begins to bother me with a stick. I have feelings of foreboding. I make as if to stand up.

'Not before we've gone through everything,' a tall man says, his biceps like treetrunks. I sit down again. Mother old one, flanked by two women and three men, goes into the house. Time passes. I'm choking, consumed on the inside. Endless nights follow upon endless nights and pile up on top of me. How many hours will mother old one need to resign herself to being dispossessed of me, to the complete shedding of me? How much more suffering will there be before she stoops down and accepts the inevitable result – the fate that will guide me to myself? '*Yooooouuuu*' sounds coming from the living room tear me away from my reflections. The crowd rushes inside. So do I.

'She is the one who stole it,' the old woman shouts as she brandishes a pair of white polyester briefs. 'I told you so, didn't I!'

'She had hidden it under her bed!' a fat woman declares.

'What a world! What a world!' another one screams putting her hand up to her head.

'Clip her wings before she goes flying off,' another one with whitened skin advises.

'Not only does she refuse to go out to work, but to top it all off she steals from her mother. Oh! What a disgrace!'

'*Hooouuu*!' the crowd cries turning towards me.

I catch their glowering looks, their yapping. Hate. Insults. Screams. My ears are going mad. My senses are bolting. I'm shaking.

I'm trembling. I need help to break up this outrageous spectacle but, subjugated by my duty as the child, my mouth recoils and pulls my body towards the street with a cry on my lips.

In my country, the foreign visitor sometimes hears the chirping of a bird. 'Life,' he thinks and lies down under his parasol, munches on some peanuts, and drinks his aperitif. Let him not make that mistake again. They are the cries of a child crushed by the earth that has sired it.

For two days and two nights I go round in circles – no goal, no place to go. Circuitous routes. Cafés. Scrubland. And nothing but my footsteps to carry me to places of perversion where street urchins and adventurers, kept by whores, are getting drunk as they invoke the sunshine of tomorrow. I am losing myself in this forbidden part of Iningué, the way some people drown in a glass of alcohol. I'm looking for the baobab in which to plant the seed of hope. A legless cripple follows me, hobbling on his crutches. Sometimes I stop in an almost empty café. I have a drink. I break down. I am in pain. I laugh to make my face blend in with those of the strangers around me. He approaches. I hear him, I feel his presence behind my back. His disabled clanking. His rancid smell. His seething heavy breath. The cold runs down my spine. Disgust? Fear? I couldn't say. I've lost the art of working myself out. I am a rotten seed. My aspirations are for an encounter with absolute blackness. Whatever my gestures might be, I roam around inside myself. I am bad luck, the child of shoddy goods. He always sits down two or three tables away from me and orders beer or wine which he drinks straight from the bottle. He wipes his mouth with the back of his hand and ogles me. He has only two fingers on each hand and white, very white teeth. They are seductive and bite down right to the bone.

On the night of the third day, he accosts me.

'I want to live a dream with you.'

I do not reply. I am a stroke of bad luck placed right in the heart of nature. A calamity, forgotten on the tree of life. 'Lame-Leg' smiles.

'The dream exists. You have to believe in it; that's all it takes.'

I am engulfed in silence. I am the shadow of a life that's lost its way. I am the body that's wilted from too much suffering. I must

108

not say a thing, for there's nothing left to connect with; nothing left to stride across to get back to my roots. At the age of sixteen, I have inhabited so many beds, with men from every country and of every colour. Day after day, all those men undulating on top of me, seeking the silhouette of their dreams . . .

'I want to love you always, forever,' Lame-Leg says. 'I'll tell you your own story. I'll describe the steepness of its slopes to you. Open your doors.'

My silence saddens him. He stays planted before me, wordlessly begging for my help, for the heat of my body to bring the desperate heights of pleasure to his senses. I am absent to his call. He moves away on his sticks.

It was then that the thing arrived, as ruthless as death. Yet, I know it well, as well as I know death itself – that fear of finding myself alone, all alone, despite the comings and goings of men. I tell myself it's time to find the tree in which to carve my name, immortalising myself once and for all.

I follow him, my mind roaming. I tell myself the story of the 'little sailor'. Ten, twenty times. It allows me to look for the elsewhere; to dream of somewhere else. I am barely aware of our taking a particular street, of going down a specific alley, of complete darkness surrounding us. How long have we been walking? Time stopped sixteen years ago between mother old one's thighs. There are only my footsteps, small or large; all my footsteps that added up must lead towards a single result – the realisation of myself.

We come into a courtyard draped in shadow. Two arms grab me. I engage my body in battle. I shout and I gesticulate but my concerted efforts anchor me in the hands of the aggressor. I bend my spine and I abandon my slip of flesh as is appropriate if the victory is to be a derisory one. He drags me into a hut, on to a mat. His steps move away. The door closes again. I look around, drunk, helpless, crowned by the mystery of the abduction perpetrated against my person.

An oppressive smell of dust surrounds me. Totems and masks hang on the walls. There are household utensils in a corner, audio-cassettes piled one on top of the other, rolled up carpets leaning against a column. In the back is a life-sized portrait of Lame-Leg.

He's wearing a red fez and a green gandoura. His chin rests on one hand. His gaze, frozen on the household items, seems to question them about the whys and wherefores. I take a step into the room, towards the photograph. I analyse it until my vision is blurred. I know the danger. I am waiting for it, immersed in destiny's fog-filled bed. 'Whatever is going to happen to you doesn't matter much,' I tell myself. 'The worst was done the day you were born sixteen years ago from between the thighs of your mother who has given you no love, who has given you nothing, not even a treeless forest where you could have hung the robes of the imagination.'

The sound of a key in the door. I turn around with my heart beating fast. The door opens and the photograph's original version appears: Lame-Leg! My nerves are taut with fear. I tense my body to form an obstacle at the hint of the movements to come. He hobbles over to me, lights his pipe and blows a huge puff of smoke in my face.

'Welcome to Lame-Leg's kingdom,' he says, holding out the two fingers of his left hand to me.

Recoiling with fear, I hesitate. Yet I know – I girlchild-woman – I know it would be wiser to trace the first curves of friendship as a welcome to survival. I know I have to flow, to adopt a fluidity under penalty of death. I entreat my hand to reach forward, to move beyond the heart of the thought and shake the mutilated hand. It obeys me. Questions become entangled in the handshake, in the man, and interrogate me. No answer. And unable to look into him, reduced to fear of that which won't declare itself, I wait, my body perplexed. I wait for the knot of speech that will break me and become a cyst in his flesh.

'What do they call you?'

I recoil and he takes the precaution of starting to laugh. I relax.

'My name is lost.'

'No problem. Here everyone is lost. I shall call your Mango. I shall pick you every season to commemorate our meeting.'

He inspects me, his eyes filming over with sex. Slowly he bends down toward our union. I turn my head away right at the moment his kiss begins to come down on my mouth.

'This place has no room for love,' I say weakly.

110

'You don't know a thing about that.'

'I can feel it.'

'Stop your inanities and follow me,' he orders. 'We're going to see the children and then,' he says throwing me a misty look of mingled flesh, 'we're going to . . .'

Without finishing his sentence, he pivots on his crutches and weaves his body towards the exit. I follow him, my heart chattering away. I couldn't begin to describe what I am feeling as we walk. I am nothing but a girlchild-woman submissive to the void and with nothing but my body to fill that void and reconcile it with the earth. Perhaps I was hoping for sunlight in the dusk, the kind that haunts time's sad dreams just before toads and owls invade the night. I couldn't say, for what dwells within me agrees with everything except the moon gliding over skins in the high chamber of love.

We make our entrance into a shed. No furnishings. Nothing but a few scattered mats. Dozens of kids dressed in rags. Some of them are sleeping, others, lying flat on the ground, seem to be waiting for the bell that will clock off the hours of life one by one. As soon as they see us they get up and bow down, before taking their place once again in the quiet ritual of prayer.

Crude images jut out over the escarpment of my thoughts. No need to lean over into the past or into the imagination to rend the veil of hope.

Even today, I still see their torn clothes, their eyes stitched through with a web of sadness and violence. Fallen shadows. How can the mango tree permit its fruit to fall before it has ripened? What crimes? What punishments? My thoughts lurch into each other, question the lunatic world with that look of suffering that calls for contemplation. I tell myself that the first word – the one that ought to announce the beginning of life and toll the bell before anything moves – that every breath should be: GIVE! GIVE! GIVE! And slide over to a throng of regulars busy signing the act of condemnation of darkness.

Lame-Leg drops down on a mat in the middle of the room, rummages through his pockets, pulls out a roll of paper and spreads it out before him.

'Dead-end!' he thunders.

A boy of about twelve separates himself from the rest. He comes closer, his eyes lowered, and puts down a few banknotes in front of Lame-Leg.

'That's all?' Lame-Leg asks peevishly.

'Yes, chief. There are good days and bad days.'

'Don't make any excuses for your failures.'

'No, chief. Seems, though, there's a shortage of everything,' he splutters. 'Fish, tomatoes, sugar. Seems there won't even be any sun any more.'

'Let it go for today. Try to do a better job tomorrow. Pig-Foot!'

'Here!' shouts a childish voice. And without leaving his place, the kid sums up: 'Twelve eggs, five kilos of intestine, three calves feet, one duck.'

'Very good,' Lame-Leg exclaims. 'Chicken-Foot!'

'Here I am, chief.'

I've already stopped listening. My body is tormented – my thoughts have no station in which to bring the train of distress to a halt. How much time is needed for dead matter to disintegrate, to loosen the earth and be returned to it? I puff out my lungs, ready to muster the breath that will go from mouth to mouth to awaken the senses, when suddenly the futility of my rebellion goes through me. There is nothing to say, nothing to be done, nothing to convey.

◆

The night is filled with my emptiness, that emptiness that walks the full length of silence, far away from speech. My eyes cut across the room and, without making a note of it, ascertain the absence of those children who have gone back to their mattresses as if born in the same shower of rain. One can live this way indefinitely, without paying attention to anything except the insipid 'tick-tock' of a watch. One minute after another, unoccupied time stretches itself beyond measure, loses its flexibility and comes back to itself, exhausted from loneliness.

'You're not saying anything.'

It's Lame-Leg. I raise my vacant eyes to him. Suddenly, the

seconds come clattering down like pebbles. I am suffocating on the flat shores of the terrible universe. I am twisting the images of terror. They arrive in hordes. Menacing clowns, they surround me, bury me. The air escapes from me. I strive to find tranquillity again; I want to attain the transparency of a soap bubble. I call for words, I command them to alleviate me, to set up the red trail of flight on my road. They present themselves, dressed in the pink harvest of my childhood, their hair like a mop of dishevelled straw. They are there, and like the housewife who knows how to keep to her schedule they clean me and set me free.

'When I was a child,' I say, 'I would refuse to go to bed. I was afraid the party would begin without me. Today, I'm no longer waiting for it.'

'All you need to do is find solace in the norm instead of dreaming.'

'That's what you all say. You legislate; you destroy.'

'I have tried to build.'

'You're nothing but an exploiter.'

'No. A conjurer, a salesman of joy, or of illusion if you prefer.'

'You're nothing but a crook. You steal what little they have from the children.'

'You've lost the art of seeing. Nothing is anything any more. All that's left for you to do is fix your eyes on the horizon and wait.'

His voice folds over the last sentence. His forehead tightens. His mouth twists as if in order to utter the words inside out. Only then do I understand that this man has slipped underneath forgotten vaults and arches to stamp the pages of happiness with his seal.

For a long while we remain facing each other, incapable of moving, resembling the shadows sculpted by the moon's belly; face to face with ourselves, as if we are statues tethered to the agonising contours of the future.

'You know,' he says suddenly, 'I've struggled for the existence of this place where childhood can live and speak. I've sacrificed everything for it. I wanted the wind to blow across their destiny so it would change its course. I wanted the child to go all the way to the death of childhood, and to be reborn divested of his parents. And nothing but love to dress him in. Today I realise that freedom is nothing but a dream. We do not exist; we do not appear on the register of the dead.'

'You exist,' I say, moved by a desire to protect him. 'Since you have feelings, you exist.'

He shrugs his shoulders.

'You don't know what you're saying.'

'You don't need to stand eye to eye with knowledge to be able to recognise things.'

'Woman's words.'

'Perhaps. That doesn't mean that between what is and what is not there are no areas of void and abyss where the illusion of life can reside.'

'You don't understand anything, you'll never understand anything! I don't want to hide. I want to know dangers other than "attempted robbery", gonorrhea or syphilis. I want to appear before God, to strangle him, and throw him in the fire. I want to walk on my hands if I feel like it. Got that?'

'I understand you're a man with a lot to say and who doesn't know where to begin. Tell me about your adventures.'

'What is it to you what the thing that oppresses and shackles me is called? In this country, anything at all can be just about anything else. All that's left to . . .'

I don't remember the rest of what he said any more. His words got lost with the entrance of a young girl, the very picture of the drop-out – the type that, shaped by absence, believes truth is a vague territory to be filled with other people, their ideas, their presence.

'Excuse me, chief, but I think it's time to go to sleep. You have to wake up early tomorrow.'

'She's right,' Lame-Leg says, grabbing his crutches and getting up with difficulty. 'Come on,' he says in my direction.

For an instant I feel like taking flight as I face his half-body. I don't want to see him inventing harmonies for me and peeling me down to my flesh in order to echo pleasure's song. I don't want any part of this wedding to be celebrated in the abjection of mutilation, amidst this pack of desolate beings. I do not want to marry this misfortune. Poor and derelict I am. But these ones who are damned, even more brutally exposed to execration, make me more

114

meagre, more uncomfortable. Suddenly I fear I'm escaping from myself, falling asleep on foreign soil, I, whose dream it is to leave, to flee from mother old one in order to put myself in the position for taking off.

But Lame-Leg is already talking. He says I am beautiful, that he'll dress me in painted canvases on the wall and make me dance to the music of his moans. And afterwards, he says, he'll put his index finger on my body's mists and, between the ripples of time, he'll show me the wounds that chain me to myself and prevent the rain, carrier of the flower's blooming. He says he understands my repugnance, but he'll teach me the secret language with which to interpret the architecture of his maimed body, and so I shall remodel his flesh to my desire.

These words break down the walls of my spirit, besiege it with disturbing images, seduce it. Already I am moving forward to the point where the senses give way. It wasn't a question of following Lame-Leg into the tomb of shared plans, but of living a nocturnal magic and waking up the next day, with the memory stuffed full of feelings, ranging all the way to the agony of death. Lame-Leg stares at me, immured in his interior eye. I tremble, as if pierced by an electric shock. A gesture is needed, a movement. I follow him into the room.

◆

That night, I devour the rites of love, pleasure in my loins. I establish my quarters there where the wave grows to excess. I explode in repeated convulsions. And I drown between the silken banners hoisted by our mingling breath. And my pleasure draws me out indefinitely, bringing words to my lips that plant love's crown in my heart.

When I wake up the next morning, there's a rope tied around my neck.

Why this knot of hatred? Why put me in a casket with a rose in my hand, when only last night he spoke to me of a long life and told me everything a man can tell a woman? I do not want to climb the tightrope of his night again. To recoil on tiptoe. Slowly, without

115

breaking anything. And my life a useless vice. I'm blocking out the noises of the compound at the threshold of my tomb. My head becomes a black hole which no lamp can illuminate. A universe rolled inside the void's kernel. Heaven has no roof any more. Earth has lost its footing. The world's chaos and its order are very distant from me. I am in the kingdom of myself, assailing myself. Thus I understand that meditating over death teaches you how to live, how to convert the void into a castle of stone.

How much time passed? I couldn't say. The door to the room opens. I close my eyes. My flesh mingles with that of death, goes past it. I don't want to be disturbed. I don't want to come back into their life, where the night puts gloves on the days to come. Yet I hear one of those angel voices that provides you with hope.

'My name is Bida, in other words "Neck-Hold". I'm supposed to take care of you, make you eat, take you out, walk you. Master's orders.'

Silence.

'You won't answer. No problem. Neck-Hold is used to the silences of grown-ups. They always miss the point.'

Silence.

'I could tickle you to make you laugh,' he says in a mischievous voice. 'Grown-ups don't like being tickled because they're afraid they might die laughing.'

Silence.

'You're not really dead, are you?'

Silence. He gets panicky, shakes me, tumbles down on me. He cries, babbling in his unhappiness. Unexpectedly, the need I feel to get lost in the labyrinths of elsewhere lessens. I take him in my arms and hug him. He pulls away. He looks at me furiously in his rags that are much too loose for his skinny body.

'You should have died,' he says, 'you should have died. At least something inside me really would have been dead. You'd be something like a mother, and I'd look at her in her coffin, in a white dress. I'd give her a flower. You understand?'

'Don't talk that way.'

'Why shouldn't I?'

116

'If you're not happy here, all you need to do is go back to your parents.'

'And then what? Here I work, I eat and nobody beats me. There the beatings never stop.'

◆

During the days that followed, I was living in a semi-conscious state. Kept on a leash by Neck-Hold, I took walks in the compound where dozens of children dressed in rags were working, laughing, copulating. They didn't look as if they had fled. They were in the land where they belonged. They were rebuilding whatever they touched. In the beginning, jealous of my privileged status with Lame-Leg, they'd make obscene gestures to discourage my advances. Sometimes I'd get a rotten tomato smack in the face. I wouldn't react. I was under the impression that I'd been stripped of everything that had weighed me down. But I do admit, there still were sudden starts of my memory, and once again I'd become the Before, attached to mother old one's stone.

Lame-Leg had installed me in his kingdom. He'd come towards night-time, hand out his orders and punishments as well. He reigned, it must be said, without any possessiveness. Once a week, the accumulated goods were divided among the members of the community. Some of the children would then go back to their parents to take them what they'd earned and return almost immediately. As for me, I was his only possession. He said that, bound to me, he was constructing fantastic dreams and chaining me to the doors of my true story. He said I was his prison of light and monsters were escaping through my bars; that calm was returning. I would listen without a word, my spirit forgotten and with absence settled inside me, until the day he suggested dusting off the theatre of his life, bringing him the resurrection of Easter, making him a child.

◆

I remember. Thunder rumbles. The spatter of rain. Lightning rips through the sky. I'm sitting on a mat, huddled up in my fear of the storm. The kids have gone back to their mattresses. It's the middle of the night. Lame-Leg has just returned and his face is preoccupied with worry. He smokes his pipe silently, but the sound of his thinking cuts through me and bothers me in my frightened state. I look at him reproachfully. I open my mouth to question him when screams resound in the courtyard: 'Thief! Informer! Kill him!' I stare at Lame-Leg, worry deep in my eyes. I half make a gesture, one that will get me closer to the information network. The door opens. Kids. A man. Bloodstained. Deep gashes cut across his cheeks. His drenched clothes gushing blood. Lame-Leg looks up at him, his eyes filled with hate.

'Is this how you've come to spy on me?'

The man doesn't answer, his eyes looking down at the puddle forming at his feet. Blackish, like chilled blood. Blood of a down-and-out God. Grown old. Seconds. Minutes. The voice rises. The questioning gets stronger.

'You gonna talk, asshole?'

The children come closer. They force him to kneel down and they tie his hands behind his back. One after the other, they urinate on him. He doesn't flinch. They empty their bladders all the way up to his mouth, the place from which words promise to emerge.

I hiccup with disgust.

'Leave him alone!'

'Be quiet!' Lame-Leg commands.

One of the children has taken out a candle. He lights it. The flame is already stroking the man's toes, the soles of his feet.

'He'll talk,' he says, 'he'll talk, the bastard. The heat will light up his memory. Right, stool pigeon . . .?'

Seconds, minutes more. The man, whose name I do not know, remains wrapped in his silence like the pit inside a fruit. And I would like, oh, how I would like him to say the first sentence – the one that will set him free. He says nothing.

I have the inevitable result at my fingertips. Lame-Leg will pronounce the sentence. Bristling with scrap metal the kids will drag the condemned man to the low shed where the instruments of torture will stitch his gown for death. They'll torment him so that he'll scream abuse at them. They'll bludgeon him. He'll scream.

Dogs will bark. Nobody will hear him. They'll hang him from the ceiling. They'll see blood gush from his nose and his mouth. They'll dab themselves with it to exorcise death. They will laugh, empty the bottle of whiskey Lame-Leg will have given them to commemorate the coming of the end. Drunk to the gills, they'll dig a hole behind the compound. They'll move the heap of flesh and rid themselves of their gruesome load.

◆

But that particular evening, despite the fact that things went without a hitch, Lame-Leg's face continues to look worried.

'What's the matter with you?'

He doesn't answer. With his gaze in some far-away place, the wings of nightbirds seem to caress his cheeks. His story attacks me. Chafed flesh. Mutilated senses. It has fallen on to the thorny path of destinies where millions of children, closed off to the world, are prattling on a cellophane planet. And I, the girlchild-woman who is desperate to find her bearings, I know it will be extinguished in a half-tone as are all stories that are too shrill. Man will no longer recognise it – it will be clogged up with soot and its breath will be silenced. He will no longer recognise it and will force me into mourning. This idea terrifies me, and makes me open my mouth wide and repeat the question.

'I think,' he says, 'the time has come for you to pay your debts.'

'I don't have a penny.'

'Money! That's the only word anyone knows any more,' he says with contempt. 'There are other things besides that, my little chick.'

'As far as we're concerned, I don't see anything else, besides my ass which you get plenty of.'

A long silence puts an end to my words. I feel the rift in his eyes; I have a foreboding of what is to come. I lower my eyes. Lame-Leg grabs his crutches, hobbles over to me and flops down on the mat. He pulls himself over on his behind, takes me in his arms. I slip away from his kiss.

'Give me a son,' he implores. 'I want so much to lay an egg in your flesh. I've loved myself so much by loving you that it's proper

119

now to crystallise it. And then too, I could have died tonight. I would have left nothing behind to perpetuate my story.'

He smiles, takes a knife out of his *boubou* and holds it out to me for the blood wedding. Distorted thoughts tear me apart – thoughts that take me back to the pure remnants of father old one rather than to the present situation. The body's memory awakens. My hands are trembling – witnesses, officiating priests at the baptism. I pick up the knife. I bring it close to Lame-Leg's finger. Fear comes into bud and my trembling becomes more apparent. The knife escapes from me.

'Cut!' Lame-Leg commands. 'I shall die and be reborn in you. I will have grown.'

But I, girlchild-woman, I suddenly know that I know. For a long time I didn't know that I knew, and here, confronted with the evidence, I know that I've always known – I do not want to clean up the landscape, I do not want to multiply myself. That is the role of the wind, of the rain. It falls to one to clear the way, to the other to sow the seed, to nourish the soil. I do not want to lend my womb to the unfurling of a life. So many children already loiter in the streets! I despise feeding the statistics. I tell him so. He bursts into sobs. He weeps loudly, the way he never wept during his childhood, in his whole life, no doubt. I take him in my arms. I describe the first child to him, and the second, and the third. I herald – I promise – the unfolding of star-poaching creatures so that he will forget his pain in the heat of his approaching fatherhood.

That night, he loves me wordlessly, his penis upright in his desire to sire a child. And I – I the woman, the child – I unfold my body to appease the turmoil of the past. When lightning runs through him, I move my hips, up and down. He cries out. I have just dealt him his most exquisite death. Without leaving him any time to catch his breath, I collect my clothes and run out into the street. I walk in the rain all night long without any sense of where I'm going. The past assails me, drumming at my temples. I laugh, I cry, seated halfway between me and myself. At dawn, I swipe a pair of panties from the shelves in the supermarket. I drag myself to the toilet. I vomit. I flush it. Exhausted, I get back to the aisles of the store. I spot a supervisor. I shake the panties under his nose and tell him I stole them. He laughs. He doesn't believe me. He says: 'She's completely out of her mind!' People gather round. Eyes full of mirth stare at me. Some people are laughing. Others comment on the hue of the particular madness which pursues me. I shrug my shoulders, stick out my tongue and let fly a spurt of spittle. They move away. I slip towards the exit . . . relieved.

I went out in the daylight again and found myself back in the place where I'd taken refuge before the brawl with mother old one. I took a very deep breath to keep myself from snivelling. I went back home. Mother old one threw herself at my feet. She wept. I didn't look at her. I gave Mala the breast. I went to find my forgotten son.

◆

Mala. From then on a silent agreement bound us. We didn't say 'good-bye' or 'see you tomorrow'. We'd leave each other as if we were never to see each other again and we'd see each other the next day in the shed. I knew, I girlchild-woman, I knew my disappearance had affected him and, furthermore, I knew we were afraid of the about-turn of destiny that would take us back in the direction of misfortune. The shortage of loving. Panic would slip in and dwell in us, creating pages of silence in which only action counted.

Mala'd come and settle himself down at my feet. I'd clean his nails, comb his hair, tell him the story of the little sailor. He'd sleep, he'd wake up, cry or utter gurgling sounds that sounded like sobs and I'd take him in my arms, cradle him and give him a mango or a piece of cake that he'd hide in his pocket. Sniffling, he'd smoke a cigarette. Only then would he kiss me and go off trundling his hoop before him.

I recall one day – a blue Mother's Day – he brings me a gift. It is a drawing – a house with a magpie at the end of the meadow.

'Is that for me?' I said, all choked up, my eyes wide-open with pleasure.

'Yes.'

I bend my face down to him, questioningly. I want to find out the reason behind the gesture – the cross signifiying happiness, matched by a motive that is valid in some way. His look clings to me. He makes buds of sunlight bloom. I exist. A gift attests to my birth. He gives me a place. He violates unhappiness. He places me inside a spoiled childhood. Gratitude is bubbling away. Its steam is wrapping me in images, filling me with emotion. I pull Mala to me and I enfold him in my arms. I want to keep him against my heart as long as possible – to purge a long long affliction of love.

'You'd make me so happy, my darling,' I say as I kiss his forehead, 'if you'd tell me why you brought me this present. Nobody ever gives me anything and I'd love it if you'd explain why you did it.'

For an instant, it seems he doesn't understand. His eyes stare at the drawing, and his fingers twist his rags as if to prevent them from giving him away, from showing a sign of mortality:

'It's so you won't dream,' he says under his breath. 'There are plenty of ghosts in there that hurt and you can't really destroy them.'

These words make their way and insert joy in me. A pact with life. The sun in my face. I allow the rain to fall from my eyes, for happiness is something to which you have to be accustomed.

The cell door opens. Anna-Claude gives a start. A soldier stands in the doorway, his silhouette broken by specks of alcohol. There are a few gashes across his face, laying bare a distant shame. A two-day growth of beard makes him look sullen. He moves into the room with tired footsteps, fractured with brutishness.

'The chief wants to see you,' he says as he belches.

Anna-Claude follows him, disquiet making her skin crawl. Torture is not what frightens her. She knows it; she has lived it; she has dreamed it. What terrifies her is what they call madness. She knows that from now on she must be explicit about it, identify it as soon as it appears, no matter from how far off. 'Blood to erase blood . . .' A crazy line of verse hides away inside her, but she must make herself forget so she won't grab the knife of fury, take off wherever her steps lead her, and strike the fist of death. Anything but that desire to celebrate the wedding with blood.

They go through a corridor. Tiny cells on either side. Bars. Grates. Bolts. Endless chains to level off every single moment of the dream. Nothing but a lesion of time open to power's vermin.

And man achieves his destiny. Prisoners everywhere, naked. Some of them, with blood on their bodies, incapable of rebellion, are deeply convinced that the torture they suffer goes back to the beginning of time. Others, emaciated, hollowed out to their very entrails, accustomed to making pacts with dread itself, look at the woman and spit obscenities at her hips. They laugh and transform the pus of their own suffering into bubbles of merriment, but their eyes, their eyes remain disconsolate.

'It's been a long time since they last saw a woman,' the soldier comments in a sleepy voice, 'if they'd grab you . . . heh, heh.'

He throws a dirty look, then hobbles on silently. They cross the courtyard. The night is clear. A few birds are breaking the peacefulness. Their piercing cries cut through the air. Anna-Claude shivers.

She has known ever since her departure that she has to take the train of gloom, to go towards chaos, in a free fall. She knows she must suffer the interrogation buried inside the heart of violence. And yet, she cannot prevent her heart from tightening, from surveying the spaces in which the idea of scientifically inflicted torture is more painful than the pain itself. How is it possible, how is it all possible? To flee from everything that is oppressive and kills. To leave with her eyes closed, to marry the universe. To depart and take along all the blemishes of the world tightly closed up inside a rubbish bag.

A fragment of glass shimmers in the lamplight of the night. Anna-Claude stops moving. She lowers her hand. She picks it up. She etches the first movement that will display whiteness. The shard burrows deep inside her palm, tears her skin. Blood flows. She tightens her lips to stop herself from crying. She starts in on her other hand. Finally she places the shard underneath her breast. She wants to sign the final act, the act of her condemnation. She hesitates; decides not to. She must wait for the dying woman in the cell to tell her story, only then will she clean her shroud at the world's tomb.

'What the fuck're you doing?' the soldier asks as he walks back to her. 'Get a move on! The Boss is waiting.'

'I have to take a piss.'

'Hurry it up.'

Anna-Claude pulls up her dress, crouches down. Urine escapes. Blood flows. A fistful of seconds in which the body is its own and gets lost. With his hands in his pockets, the soldier waits. He can do nothing other than watch the eyes of time, so that Anna-Claude, relieved of her discomfort, will entwine herself in words and deposit her secrets in the sludge that will lead to someone's promotion. But the question is which promotion? That of Humanity or that of man? Centuries will be needed for the executioner to understand he is the prisoner of his victim. Seconds are needed for the cry of pain to rise to heaven!

◆

A house surrounded by barbed wire. The gate is open. The door is, too. He brings her into a room. It is spacious. The walls, in a virginal colour, stink of fresh paint. In the centre there's a table, an old typewriter, registration books and two chairs. A man stands at the back. His short legs are floating in a shapeless pair of trousers. His unbuttoned shirt shows a stomach that is growing stout, laced with tiny tufts of hair. His steel-rimmed glasses make him look like an intellectual. As soon as the soldier spots him, he stands to attention.

'Here is the prisoner, chief,' he says.

'Fine. You may go.'

He goes out, closing the door behind him. Anna-Claude is trembling. Slowly, the chief comes closer. He examines her, his eyes like knives.

'I like you,' he declares. 'I'm going to help you get out of here.'

She remains mute. He points to a chair. She collapses, her mind befuddled. He sits down facing her. With a nervous gesture, he inserts paper into the typewriter.

'Last name, first name, age, profession.'

'Girlchild-woman, black, seventeen, whore some of the time.'

He looks at her, ominously. She's making a fool of him, he knows it; she's challenging him. He, who had so carefully prepared his interrogation! No. He will not resort to rage. Better to gain some time. He takes out a cigarette, lights it, takes a puff and leans back in his chair with his eyes on the ceiling.

'Your grandparents enslaved mine. Your country strips mine bare. You're fucking around with me.'

'You've been biting your own tail, all by yourself,' she says and bursts out laughing. He doesn't understand, he's losing track of where he's heading. He says: 'Explain.' She goes on laughing and says that the world's ugliness is tickling her. She shows him her bloody hands. She tells him it's the Germans who did that, as they once did to the Sarahs and the Rachels and to her mother. She says blood is necessary, always more blood – to wash out the hard luck of Blacks, Jews, Arabs – but that as we wait, a seventeen-year-old child, locked up in a cell, will fail to climb back up the neck of the funnel.

She talks; she tells the story. No queen is more eloquent, no mad

125

woman either. When she notices the chief's mind go blank, his silence, she realises that centuries will be needed before words can cross the night to reach him draped in daylight. She knows it would take much time for reason to drip into his veins . . . She stops speaking.

'I'm glad you're quieting down,' he says in a lacklustre voice. 'Now we'll be able to talk, my dear.'

'I have nothing to say.'

'That's what you all say. But then the tongues start wagging. You'll see.'

'I have nothing to say,' she repeats with energy.

'You've got death hanging over you.'

'I don't give a damn. There's nobody left inside me.'

Seriousness seals their mouths. Anna-Claude's lips droop. Her expression locks itself into distress, reduces it to its concrete form.

'You are of no interest to us,' the chief says, breaking the silence. 'There's a woman with you – a dangerous criminal – picked up with a group of forgers. She's the one we must have.'

'I am she.'

'Stop your idiocies!' he shouts and pounds his fist on the table. 'Let out all that you know, then we'll set you free.'

'I am she,' she repeats.

The chief gets up and plants himself in front of her, menacingly. He shouts. Sweat beads on his forehead. He says that people of her kind are killing the world and it would be good to hand them over to the gentle care of flies. He says that if she's determined to remain silent, so much violence will emerge from him that they'll be forced to register her loss and soon everyday life will have surrounded her with indifference. He talks on and describes the circle of violence, blood's voluptuousness. Anna-Claude is silent, and as long as she remains silent, he becomes more irritated. Yet he'd promised himself to stay calm, yet . . . Finally, worn out, the words fall silent by themselves. In his fury, there's a sudden luminous opening. There's nothing left but fornication to bring the woman to reason.

The thought having barely been articulated, he starts up the love machine. Hands. Fingers. Mouth. An association of every fibre imaginable for pleasure. He makes love to her. And all the while that he's devoting himself to her flesh, he speaks, whispering questions. Who is she? Where does she come from? What has Tanga said? But no clam has ever been so silent. She's learning about the flight of survival. Her body absents itself, overtakes its shadow. No sex. No breasts. No nose. The void. Her mouth alone forms a strange independent litany.

> ACCUMULATE SILENCES
> ACCUMULATE SILENCES
> I AM ILLUSION
> I AM MADNESS

He lets go of her – he's furious. He slaps her hard, a volley of slaps. She brings a hand up to her cheek. It's not the pain which hurts her but the absence of sky.

'What did you say?' he says loudly.

'Nothing.'

'You're lying!'

'I'm learning the language of love. It has no words. You can't chain it up like your mother's dog.'

He looks at her with terror in his eyes. His entire being is channelled in this gaze. A sob rises in his throat.

'Forgive me,' he says. 'This morning I lost the dog my mother left me on her deathbed. It was all I had of hers. You understand?'

'Some people lose their dog, others their child.'

'Shut up!'

She realises he's suffering and wants to make him suffer. She bursts out laughing. She begrudges him nothing, except the dog removed from his affection.

When she gets back to the cell, daylight stands in the doorway and Tanga's heart, about to take its leave, is beating only faintly. She takes her pulse. She wipes her forehead. She lies down against her. She knows that Tanga was waiting for her in order to die – open, offering herself, so she could give her words to speak before crossing the borders and lying down full length as a still-life. She knows that from now on no blow, no grace will be able to prevent the girlchild-woman from fertilising the earth, from nurturing space.

127

Then, there are her dead ones, too. They will anticipate the shadow of fear that had partitioned her off in dreams. They'll invalidate every door and every bolt. They'll yield one by one, shatter before the injunctions of death. Love the blade of love, Anna-Claude will brandish you! She will shout you out! Belch. Black. She will startle her audience. She will hold her silhouette erect in the emptiness. She will finally expose you. And man will retrieve you. He will arrange you. He will classify you. In the yellow pages of dead knowledge. This is how Anna-Claude will destroy you. But she doesn't know that. In order to know that, she would have had to know the frozen state of conscience which inhabits the world. She would have had to be born with other eyes, would have had to monitor her steps so as not to lose her dream. She should have . . .

'Did they hurt you?' Tanga asks.

'It was nothing, just sex.'

'Where man lives only time can tamper with suffering. I feel my body escaping, and yet I want to live a little bit longer, to enclose the world in an ivory tower and increase the impression of happiness. Do you understand?'

'You needn't be afraid of anything. I exist therefore you shall be.'

Tanga smiles and opens her mouth – she wants to add some words. Anna-Claude forces her to be quiet and tells her it's time to continue her Story, to call up her dead, so that she may carry and validate her beyond the world.

'I'll be too heavy,' the dying woman says. 'You won't know how to retrace my path. You are too old.'

'I'm always fifteen, when I love.'

'They'll be torturing you with questions.'

'So?'

'They'll whip you.'

'That's my problem.'

'One piece of advice. Sign everything they ask you to sign. You must always sign to get some peace.'

Anna-Claude watches her, looking as if her mind is somewhere else. She knows anguish is there but that she must ever and always work at making the light dawn. She closes her eyes then says to

Tanga in a restrained voice: 'Continue your story. It will guide me; it is what you must bequeath to me.'

Then silence filtered into the word, into a space where consciousness did not become obliterated as the earth is obliterated along the road upon which men tread.

Mala and I decide to adopt a dog. Didn't they come first, before men? Don't they help in creating the illusion of a family? We chose one like ourselves: cursed and maimed. No ears left and only half a tail. Early on, we hunt down his fleas. We tie him to a tree. We rub down his sparse coat with a brush. We pour out water for him. He howls. We continue. We give him bones and scraps. He puts on some weight. We decide he's too good looking to be simply trampling the soil. After suffering the damage of deprivation, shouldn't enchantment be made to last? If we've been banned from the sunlight, our dog must have his place in the sun. We work towards that end. We steal some slippers from a supermarket. We put them on him. He protests with his head, with his muzzle. He tries to walk. We notice he can't figure out any more which foot to put in front of which. He begins with the right back paw, then the left front paw. We laugh. We've just discovered a new way of making a living.

We take him to the public squares. We make him do his trick. People are laughing while one of us swipes their purse. We go to the white section of town at tea-time. We're not allowed in there but our little show appeals to the kids. They come with their cakes, their stuffed bread rolls and their toys. We show them the feat and they say: 'Do it again!' We answer: 'You'll have to pay.' They give us things to eat. Sometimes we surreptitiously replace the cheese with soap and then give them back their sandwich. They bite into it and spit it out. We laugh. We rediscover the basic knowledge of children.

Throughout that period, I felt something akin to happiness. Foot-wreck was my son. He clung to my chest. He'd say: 'I'm hungry, Ma.'

I'd take out one breast. He'd suckle. He'd fall asleep. In my happiness, I'd worry about his. At one and the same time, we were each other's saviours and the evil eye that lay in wait for us. I knew

130

it. But I was prepared to do anything in order to put my face to the skylight that promised deliverance.

Mother old one wouldn't let herself be supplanted. She was like those thousands of leeches teeming in the swamps of Iningué. A tamed leech. It was by suction that I had hold over her, my mother leech. I gave her my blood. Just enough to keep her alive – to keep myself alive. I'd give her the money from our pilfering. She'd shove it inside her blouse with a look of disgust, wipe her clammy hands on her *kaba* and be off to cling to my sister. 'Go ahead, Ma! Get bogged down, go astray! Maybe only then will I have a chance of understanding life and finding the lake of destiny again!'

A memory. It's afternoon. It's very hot. I'm sunk in a chair underneath the verandah. I notice heavy breathing next to me. I open one eye. Mother old one stands there, bundled up in a faded *kaba*, with her hands on her hips. She's smiling – I've never noticed how yellow her teeth are. She pulls her *kaba* up way over her thighs and leans over to me until her mouth is next to my ear:

'Your cunt has become a stone wall.'

'A nest of lamentation,' I say.

'Damn you!'

I shrug my shoulders. I fix my eyes on her body. Her fleshy lips. Her eyes overcome with hate. I would have liked to tell her that Mala, the child with the wrecked feet, has closed my genitals with his raw tenderness. I say nothing. I must say nothing to protect myself from the smack her hands are itching to deliver. She paws the ground, whinnies a few threats and moves away, her back stiff.

◆

I didn't have any more nightmares. Just a few ghosts. Sometimes they'd stay away from my nights. No more nocturnal wandering. Nothing but the body lying down, decayed in sleep. I was becoming bored – I'd call for them, for I'd begun to understand they were the catalyst blowing me towards heaven. Time was passing. Seated between two chairs, I owned it. I was almost happy. Yet, I knew that the red blackness of misfortune was not far away. I saw it prowl around me, pounding the streets on either side of me. I didn't dare imagine the worst, for I, girlchild-woman, I knew I'd be in the right. I was pursuing ghastly thoughts. I was clothing myself in hope in order to defy my fears. I had the temerity to count on love reducing the effects of disaster, their destruction. I forgot that misfortune is the son of happiness and that, rekindled in its heart, it awaits the propitious moment to flatten it, inch by inch.

◆

On that April morning it is raining. Barely a few sprinkles, but draping the sky with a cloak of mourning. The air smells as it does after it has rained. I go over to our shed with a foreboding of disaster in my body. The mud sticks to my feet, weighing me down. I keep going, my nerves on edge. I pass people as if they were shadows. They greet me, I nod my head, words have dried up. I arrive at the shed. Mala isn't there. I sit down and try to give substance to my dreams. In vain. The minutes trickle by, making me as cold as ice. I doze off.

When I open my eyes, night is about to fall; it's humid. I go out, my spirit trembling. I run towards Mala, my child. I cut across the fields to recapture love. Out of breath, I arrive in front of his house. I go in without knocking. The air reeks of sweat and vomit. A kerosene lamp is burning and lights up dozens of faces around the place. Some are sleeping. Others are getting drunk. With her scalp shaven, Mala's grandmother sits enthroned behind a demi-john of Bako which she serves with much clicking of the tongue. I go over to her. She raises her nest of wrinkles and looks at me with covetousness as thick as slime.

'Finally!' she says. 'I've been waiting a long time for you, my girl.'

'No time, Ma. Where is Foot-wreck?'

'He's hatching his worms,' she says pointing to a curled up shape in a corner. I go over to him. I touch his forehead which is clammy with sweat. Weary, he opens his eyes. He recognises me, smiles and asks me to tell him the story of the little sailor. I obey, the words heavier than stones. I know how the child is suffering from the worms cutting into his intestines. And all night long I stay by his side and even pray, though I've never known where to send my soundwaves. To luminous angels of the shadow or to the dark ones of the light? I pray as I move from bead to bead on the rosary which Mala's grandmother has lent me. Occasionally, a sharp pain wakes him. He puts his hand on his belly and vomits worms. I clean up. Terror is living inside me. The rancid smell of vomit as well.

It's barely daylight. Weakened, I hoist Mala on my back. I walk with difficulty, eyes fixed on my destination. I turn the words over and over in my head – words I must say to convince the doorman of the clinic to let us in. I walk on, persuaded that his familiarity with the sun and the moon will make him give in and induce him to open the door to recovery for us. But the words I prepared become tarnished with each step I take. My mouth is full of hollow-sounding words like Goodness and Beauty . . . Logic is fleeing from me. With each thought, I stray further away from myself.

A shadow detaches itself and is walking by my side. I turn my head. An old man. Tall. Thin. With a dog dripping blood that he is holding at the end of an improvised leash. He smiles at me. He says he quickened his steps to walk with me. He adds: 'The road is less hard-going when there are two.' I agree.

As we walk he tells me about his dog. They've known each other for twelve years. He's always beaten him to give himself the illusion of life, to feel on top of things. Today someone else has beaten his dog – an arrow in his ear. He doesn't want him to die, this old carcass, not before he himself does, for that desertion – nothing new in his life – would force him to look towards the opening, the hole.

'What'll become of me?' he asks as he swallows his tears.

'Nothing, sir. Nothing. The dead are like the living. Always the same defects, the same ills.'

'You're right, my girl,' he says after a moment's reflection. 'The earth is old and round.'

◆

The hospital. A line of people several metres long. People everywhere, men, women, children, polished to the gills, their eyes staring at the ground, wait for the moment of light when time will grant their prayer. Then the gate will open and, as one man, they'll rush forward towards the white jacket that will deliver healing.

The moment did not come. All day long the crowd waits. Some sitting down, others standing, each one locked into his own cage, united by the same stare – the one you fix on another person you think is sicker than yourself. Just to tell yourself there are those more unfortunate than you. I get up several times with the sun beating on my skull. I go to the doorman and, worn to the bones, give him my speech. He doesn't listen. He remains seated on a stool, his hands on his knees. He looks at his fingers, cluttered with furuncles and cracks. He is concentrating so hard that it seems he has forgotten us. Deafness is the art of hearing too much. I'd never thought about that.

I come; I go; I moisten Mala's forehead to destroy death. Is there a real danger here? I avoid that thought. I count the cars that pass with their wheels screeching. I ask the sun to blaze a little less. There's nothing to do, nothing to take. The only thing left is to open one's door to the wait so that, jarred, it will bring tomorrow.

Towards the end of the day, the event was born. The hospital gate opened and poured its patients out into the street – those who'd suffered accidents, the tubercular, the epileptics, the lepers, the syphilitics, the malaria patients. Those who can't walk are carried on stretchers or on the backs of men. Everywhere the odours of decay and death mixed with the odours of the day's end. I control myself. I question an old man about what's happening. He raises a face like Nicodemus towards me and says: 'He is resurrected. He sets us free and heals us. I'm going to be young again!'

He gets lost in the crowd, limping away.

I, girlchild-woman, I have a hole in my head. There's nothing to understand, it's simply a case of following the road that leads to recovery. I hoist Mala on my back and follow the procession. Men come out from everywhere and join us. One-armed, one-eyed men, beggars, blind people, cripples. And many more, even the healthy, poor and rich. From time to time a woman throws herself on the ground, tears her clothes and shrieks: 'I've sinned against you, Lord!' She lists her cuckolded husbands, her poisoned children, and the

134

co-wives on whom she's put a spell. Chaos. Those who collapse are trampled. Rumours are making the rounds. They say that 'He' is a kind of God who's come from heaven knows where, from a land that has no day where there's ice everywhere. They say that 'He' heals all kinds of diseases and they've even seen sterile seventy-year-old women give birth to a chubby-cheeked baby with four teeth in its mouth, the very next day. They say . . . I listen, I invoke the wind that will right the helm and will straighten the flags of deliverance.

We go up a slope. The heat is stultifying. A leaden grey sky. We enter a stadium guarded by dozens of policemen; they're directing the crowd. There's a howl. The crowd storms the stadium.

A seat placed in the middle of the field is on the only unoccupied bit of ground. All over the place the sick flop down, lie down, kneel down. Serious faces, almost worried. Some of them take plastic bags full of manioc sticks and pistachio cakes out from their *boubous* and bite into them with gusto. They explain that they come from far off, from the other end of the country. The miracles of Lord von Deutschman have long talons.

How much time went by before the Lord entered the stadium? I couldn't say.

'Oooooooh!' the crowd shouts raising its arms toward heaven. I realise he must be there. I turn around. My chest is one big knot of hope, a tremendous line of what is to come, impossible to be expressed in words. Lord von Deutschman is tall and blond, a good-natured man, with the broad gestures of a Lord. He slides rather than walks in his clothes that are white with mystery to erase the coming shadow.

Lord von Deutschman climbs on to the platform, raises his arms to heaven, and with an appropriate expression on his face, he then says:

'Dear brothers, dear sisters, let us praise the resurrected Christ!'

'Hallelujah!' screams the crowd.

'He sets us free and heals us!'

'Hallelujah!'

'Let he who does not hear listen to me. Let he who does not see look at me!'

'Hallelujah!'

135

I shout; I scream my head off; I want my voice to rise, to scrape away evil, to clean the air. Separated from myself, I shout out. From time to time you hear a voice exclaim: 'I see, I see, thank you Lord' or 'I hear, I hear, I hear . . . I am healed'. And I keep on shouting 'hallelujahs'. A man is going around through the crowd collecting money in a large bag. People give whatever they have: money, jewellery, watches. Latecomers arrive running, sweating, smelly. Small bags of change under their arms which they give for more blessings. I give a one hundred-franc coin, the only one in my possession. I would have liked so much to give more! Maybe then . . .

The sky has opened up in the meantime and a fine rain is churning up the soil. I lean over towards Mala to mark the instant that he'll tear himself off the ground and shout: 'I have been healed, I have been healed!' I touch him; he doesn't react. I call his name, he doesn't answer. Dead. I've just begun to understand . . . Money! Money! Forged or genuine! I had to find its tree! I looked for several days. I found men who transform reams of paper into banknotes. I followed them. The police came. You understand?

'Let your heart fall silent. Be quiet – be quiet,' Anna-Claude says breaking the thread of the story. 'That's all you need to do, let your heart fall silent, be quiet.'

136

I shout, I scream my head off, I want my voice to rise, to scrape away evil, to clean the air. Separated from myself, I shout out. From time to time you hear a voice exclaim, 'I see, thank you Lord,' or 'I hear, I hear, I hear...' I am healed. And I keep on shouting 'hallelujahs', A man is going around through the crowd collecting money in a large bag. People give whatever they have; money.

Daytime. Ashen and muddy as the future. A woman wrapped in a grey *kaba* crosses the prison courtyard with long steps. With her hair braided close to her scalp and her grey *kaba*, she gives the impression of frailty disguised as strength. She greets a policeman with a familiar gesture, slips him a five hundred-franc note. He thanks her, shoves the money into his pocket and precedes her down a long corridor where hearts are held captive by fear. Only a few stares from behind steel bars convey the Babel of life. They end up in front of an isolated cell. The policeman opens it. A young woman. Redhead or blonde, as far as the little window with its rickety filtered patch of light shows. She's hunched over, her chin on her knees. No outside sound seems to be haunting her surroundings any more. The woman in the grey *kaba* kneels down before her.

'My girl. Tell me, what have they done with my daughter,' she groans.

'Your daughter?'

'Yes, my daughter. She was locked up here with you. Tell me . . .'

'I am your daughter.'

'Not you,' the woman says in an irritated voice, 'my daughter, Tanga.'

'That's me . . .'

'Leave her alone,' the cop intervenes. 'She's completely off her rocker. We'll go look elsewhere.'

The woman in the grey *kaba* gets up and moves away towards the exit with lifeless steps. Just as she is about to cross the threshold, Anna-Claude looks at her, staring, dense, then says:

'You have killed us both, Madame.'